ROUTLEDGE LIBRARY EDITIONS: FAMILY

Volume 9

FAMILY AND SCHOOL

FAMILY AND SCHOOL

DAPHNE JOHNSON
AND
ELIZABETH RANSOM

LONDON AND NEW YORK

First published in 1983 by Croom Helm Ltd

This edition first published in 2023
by Routledge
4 Park Square, Milton Park, Abingdon, Oxon OX14 4RN

and by Routledge
605 Third Avenue, New York, NY 10158

Routledge is an imprint of the Taylor & Francis Group, an informa business

© 1983 Daphne Johnson and Elizabeth Ransom

All rights reserved. No part of this book may be reprinted or reproduced or utilised in any form or by any electronic, mechanical, or other means, now known or hereafter invented, including photocopying and recording, or in any information storage or retrieval system, without permission in writing from the publishers.

Trademark notice: Product or corporate names may be trademarks or registered trademarks, and are used only for identification and explanation without intent to infringe.

British Library Cataloguing in Publication Data
A catalogue record for this book is available from the British Library

ISBN: 978-1-032-51072-9 (Set)
ISBN: 978-1-032-53691-0 (Volume 9) (hbk)
ISBN: 978-1-032-53697-2 (Volume 9) (pbk)
ISBN: 978-1-003-41318-9 (Volume 9) (ebk)

DOI: 10.4324/9781003413189

Publisher's Note
The publisher has gone to great lengths to ensure the quality of this reprint but points out that some imperfections in the original copies may be apparent.

Disclaimer
The publisher has made every effort to trace copyright holders and would welcome correspondence from those they have been unable to trace.

Family and School

DAPHNE JOHNSON AND ELIZABETH RANSOM

CROOM HELM
London and Canberra

© 1983 Daphne Johnson and Elizabeth Ransom
Croom Helm Ltd, Provident House, Burrell Row,
Beckenham, Kent BR3 1AT

British Library Cataloguing in Publication Data

Johnson, Daphne
   Family and school
   1. Parent-teacher relationships—England
   2. Education, Secondary—England
   I. Title   II. Ransom, Elizabeth
   373.41   LC225.33

   ISBN 0-7099-2236-1

The research on which this book is based
was supported by a grant from the
Department of Education and Science.
The views expressed in the book are
those of the researchers and should not
be taken to represent the views or
policies of the Department.

Printed and bound in Great Britain by
Biddles Ltd, Guildford and King's Lynn

CONTENTS

Acknowledgements

PART I:	INTRODUCTION AND BACKGROUND	
Chapter One:	A new enquiry into home/school relations	1
Chapter Two:	Themes in the study of home/school relations	18
PART II:	THE NEW RESEARCH	
Chapter Three:	Before the secondary school years	31
Chapter Four:	Parents and secondary school teachers in contact	50
Chapter Five:	Parents and teenagers	70
Chapter Six:	What the school asks of parents	83
Chapter Seven:	Home, school and the welfare agencies	97
PART III:	SUMMARY AND REFLECTIONS	
Chapter Eight:	Family and secondary school - the relationship re-assessed	117
Appendix:	Methods of the research study	129
Bibliography		142
Index		145

ACKNOWLEDGEMENTS

The Department of Education and Science provided funding for the Schools, Parents and Social Services project, carried out by members of the Educational Studies Unit at Brunel University, under the direction of Professor Maurice Kogan. The home interviews with parents on which this book is chiefly based formed part of the fieldwork for that project. Other aspects of the project are reported in *Secondary Schools and the Welfare Network* (Johnson et al, 1980).

The authors are grateful to Maurice Kogan for the encouragement and advice he has contributed to this account of the parental interviews, and for comments by Maurice Kogan, Len Davis and other colleagues on an earlier draft.

Katherine Bowden played an equal part, with the two authors, in the interviewing of parents. Her contributions to the fieldwork and concurrent research discussions, and to preliminary work on this book are warmly acknowledged.

The patience, acumen and secretarial stamina of Sonia Leggett and Mary Furnell have been invaluable.

Daphne Johnson
Elizabeth Ransom

Part I

Introduction and background

Chapter One

A NEW ENQUIRY INTO HOME/SCHOOL RELATIONS

There is no shortage of advice to parents on how they should bring up their children, and what their relationship should be with the schools their children attend. More rarely heard is the parent's voice of experience on the stages of family life and how the children's school life is seen from the family point of view.
In this book we offer a perspective on the secondary school years from the standpoint at home. Our informants are the fathers and mothers of the children attending four comprehensive schools in outer London. This new interview material prompts a re-examination of conventional wisdom on the subject of home/school relations.
Throughout the twentieth century, parents and educators have been gripped in a shared responsibility for children's schooling. Parents have been required to put their children to school, and education authorities have been required to provide the places for them. But over and above the statutory partnership, the idea of a relationship of contact and cooperation between home and school has gradually evolved. The stages through which the debate about home/school relations has passed are discussed in some detail in the next chapter, but perhaps the most influential contribution was made by the Plowden Report in the late 1960s. "Children and their Primary Schools" (HMSO 1967) stressed the advantages of close contact and understanding between parents and teachers, in fostering the development of children. The pattern of relations advocated by Plowden has become the implicit model for expectations about a desirable home/school partnership throughout the compulsory school years.
Our purpose in writing this book is to urge the reconsideration of taken-for-granted assumptions about the appropriate relationship between home and secondary school. Research with parents of secondary school children gives grounds for new thinking about the partnership of family and school.

A new enquiry

Our main contentions are:

1. there are legitimate differences in the expectations which parents and teachers have about the objectives of contact between home and school;
2. teachers, for the most part, expect parents to interact with the secondary school on the basis of a primary school model of home/school relations;
3. the family's approach to the secondary school is in the context of earlier primary school experience. But the moment of transfer may also be the moment for reviewing future behaviour and attitudes;
4. primary school teachers' contacts with parents are based on the recognition of the dependency of the child. But during the secondary school years the relationship between child and parent is rapidly changing. The dynamics of family life and relationships strongly influence the degree and type of involvement which parents have with their children's secondary schools;
5. the success of home/school cooperation tends to be evaluated by teachers on the basis of parents coming to the school. But parents who do not come to the secondary school are not necessarily apathetic about their children's education and development. Many home-based forms of parental support and interest are invisible to teachers.

The discussions which we have had with parents of secondary schoolchildren have also provided insights into some more detailed aspects of the links between home and school. It is clear, for example, that a family's criteria for the choice of secondary school for a child are considerably more complex than the 1980 Education Act and accompanying political debate suggest.

Once the child has joined the school, our research also indicates, the pattern of parental response to school invitations relates to what parents think the event is about, rather than the purpose which the school claims for it. Attendance at many school events will depend on whether they evoke the central concern of parents with their own child. But the parents' involvement with the school is not totally contingent upon the child. It may be the child's membership of the school which legitimates parents' membership of the PTA, for example, but PTA involvement may be evaluated as a social activity in its own right, in which parenthood is no more than the passport to entry.

Another aspect of home/school liaison on which our research throws light is the very limited extent to which the school acts as an intermediary for welfare agencies. Nor, it

A new enquiry

seems do agency practitioners themselves stand out to parents as linking figures between school and home. Education welfare officers, educational psychologists, school-based social workers are all to some extent intended to bridge the gap between family and school, but this aspect of their achievements seems limited.

Later chapters will discuss in detail the points of view which parents expressed about all these matters. But first some account must be given of the parents themselves, and the research to which they contributed.

CONTEXT OF THE RESEARCH STUDY

The 109 home interviews on which this book is chiefly based were carried out in adjacent sectors of the boroughs of Hillingdon and Hounslow. But these encounters were planned, and are interpreted, in the context of a more wide ranging research design. A three year study of the relationships between secondary school, the homes of pupils and a number of welfare and control agencies was funded by the Department of Education and Science, from 1974 to 1977. The schools' and agencies' share in the research evolved as an extended collaborative research dialogue with 120 teachers and agency practitioners working in or linked in some way with four large comprehensive schools.

The way in which the research dialogue with schools and agencies was developed and sustained is fully described in "Secondary Schools and the Welfare Network" (Johnson et al 1980). Individually, and later in working groups, teachers, education welfare officers, social workers, educational psychologists, child psychiatrists and many other agency practitioners explored with researchers the practice and the implications of their working roles for their relationships with one anothers and with their pupils/clients and their families.

The focus of enquiry with teachers, social workers and other agency practitioners was the work by which they earned their living. All the research discussions took place, appropriately, at the work base, be it school, clinic, civic centre or area office. But in moving on to explore the relationship between family and school, the researchers approached a task which differed in many respects from that offered by a study of schools and agencies.

In planning a research approach to parents we were aiming to make contact with private individuals in private life. The appropriate place to talk to parents was obviously in the home itself, even though home interviews can prove difficult to arrange and to conduct. Our eventual experience in carrying out these home interviews is fully discussed in the Appendix which also gives an account of how the sample of parents was

A new enquiry

selected.

THE RANGE OF PARENTS APPROACHED

Most written and verbal comment about parents by educationists treats parents as homogeneous group. Teachers are less prone than administrators to presume that parents are all alike, but their models of categorisation tend to be broad. Our research aim in the eliciting of parents' points of view was to dispel the brisk stereo-typing and 'lumping together' of parents practised by some teachers, and reveal some of the diversity of parenting which is to be found within a small and relatively homogeneous area of greater London.

To fulfil this aim, it was essential we did not restrict our enquiries to those parents with whom the school was in frequent contact, whether as 'model' parents, members of the PTA and to be seen at every school function, or as 'problem' parents, regularly in dispute with the school. We wanted to design a sample which might include actively pro and anti school parents, but which would also bring us into contact with parents about whom the school knew little, parents who might exemplify or call into question the teachers' stereo-type of the 'apathetic vast majority'.

In the event, the 109 families we contacted included closely-knit and broken families, parents with high expectations of what secondary education could offer their children and others who saw it as a temporary and often avoidable interruption of their child's real life. Some of the parents seemed motivated to take part in the research by their scorn for their child's school, and others by their hearty approval of it. What we gleaned from the interviews was not only the views of parents about the school and their own role as parents of secondary school children. We also learned a great deal about the diversity of life styles and family organisation in large and small families, families of limited or more ample means and accommodation, and of varying ethnic origins.

Since one of our concerns was to draw out some of the differences amongst families coming from what may appear to an outsider to be a homogeneous group, it is now difficult for us to characterise the parents in our sample as if they formed a single collectivity. Nevertheless, a description of some of their salient characteristics may help to place the interviews in context.

The bulk of the parents would be occupationally classified as working class with only a few such as bank clerks or clerical officers coming into the lower middle class category. There was a preponderance of husbands and wives who themselves had grown up in the locality, and even incomers had mostly been settled locally for some years at the time of interview.

None of our sample of parents had been to university in Britain, and few, with the exception of immigrant Asian families, had engaged in extended education. For nearly every family, the educational achievements of their children were outstripping the parents' own educational attainments.

Few parents travelled far to work. Employment opportunities in West London were quite good at the time of study, which may have minimised the need to travel, and incoming families had no doubt been attracted by the buoyant labour market. Parents expressed a preference for their own children finding local jobs.

Most families lived in council estates dating from the thirties and fifties, and the few families in private homes tended to be occupying houses of similar age and appearance, that is brick-built linked or terraced housing or grey pebble-dashed semi-detached. The nuclear family was the most common household unit. Given the stage of the developmental cycle of family composition when children are of secondary school age, this was to be expected, though we noticed that we seemed to be encountering a number of older parents. In many instances, this was related to a large family, rather than to delayed child bearing.

What all parents had in common was that they had children at one of four outer London comprehensive schools. These schools, which have been described in detail elsewhere, (Johnson et al, 1980) were all local institutions of long standing, reorganised for the most part from an earlier secondary modern form.

THE HOME INTERVIEWS

Our interviews were loosely structured as to content, and once embarked upon, most of them lasted for an hour or more. (An outline of interview content is given in the Appendix.) Meanwhile, family life flowed on around us. During many of the interviews other family members and sometimes the informants themselves prepared meals, did washing, ironing or dressmaking, sun-bathed, gardened or carpentered or nursed sick children. Television programmes provided a counterpoint to the interview dialogue, and younger children played or complained around us. By contrast, some of the interviews, especially those with shift workers and full-time housewives, took place in the quietness of an empty house during the morning and early afternoon. On a few occasions father and mother together arranged an evening appointment with the researcher, when with other family members banished, they could settle down for a proper talk.

To give some feel of the diversity of these research encounters, and the family situation they disclosed, we offer five vignettes which recall particular interviews.

A new enquiry

Interview with Mrs. Morgan
From outside, the Morgan's home looked impoverished and shabby. Two broken-down cars stood outside the house, which was in a remote street of a local authority housing estate. The neighbourhood seemed to have been planned on the 'backwater' principle, developing a piece of formerly waste ground. There were only two roads out of the estate, so people walking or driving in its streets were never on their way through to anywhere else - they either lived in or were coming to visit one of the council houses.

Mrs. Morgan, in her mid-forties, was fat and husky-voiced. She had five children, and it seemed to be she who played the major role in their upbringing. Her husband, she explained, had a 'very bad temper if he loses it - a bit violent - so he'd rather be easy with them'. Mr. Morgan was not seen during the interview, but he was evidently the family breadwinner. Mrs. Morgan did not go to work.

Inside the house, space was at a premium and it was difficult to see where the interview could take place. The kitchen was being redecorated and was unusable. In the living room the curtains were drawn and several children were watching television in the twilight. The other room downstairs was the eldest son's bedroom. Mrs. Morgan and the interviewer sat down on the bed, and began to talk about the children and their schools.

The three oldest Morgan children were all boys, now aged 19, 14 and 12. The eldest boy, who had attended a nearby secondary modern school, had been at work for several years, apprenticed in the furniture trade. The middle boy was at a grammar school, and the youngest of the three was a first year pupil in one of the comprehensive schools participating in the research project. This school was quite a long way from where the Morgans lived.

The fourth and fifth children were girls, aged 10 and 7. 'I had to work hard to get a girl', Mrs. Morgan commented. They attended a primary school very close to hand.

The Morgans had their work cut out to keep the family going financially, but this had not reduced Mrs. Morgan to an attitude of laissez faire about the children's behaviour, education or future lives. Thoughtful and articulate, she was by no means convinced of the value of extended education but her ideas about motherhood, child development and an appropriate relationship between home and school were clearly thought through.

In her view, the maternal role when schooldays began was to ease the child from dependency on mother into a developing relationship with the teacher, still having confidence that mother was reliably in the background. From then on, how children got on at school would be chiefly a product of how they got on with the teacher, and their own abilities and enthusiasms. Mrs. Morgan would help where she could with spelling and general knowledge, but on the whole school work was for school, and she did not really believe in much homework. The middle son's acceptance of a grammar school place had to be very much his own choice, backed by his teachers' recommendation. The Morgans had signed a paper to say he could stay there until he was 18, but it was the boy himself who had to live with the consequence of this.

Nevertheless there had been parental intervention in the choice of secondary school to the extent that the eldest boy's experience at the local school had ruled it out as a possibility for the younger children. No matter how they were raised at home, children's friends and school companions were very influential. Local children's behaviour had offered a bad example, so the younger children must be sent to schools further afield.

Geographical distancing of the schools, combined with Mrs. Morgan's sense of an appropriate emotional distance as children grew older, combined to minimise the parents' contacts with the children's secondary schools, whether grammar or comprehensive. 'Both the cars are off the road at the moment', Mrs. Morgan said euphemistically, 'and it's a long way.'

Still, she had gone to the comprehensive school for an open evening when her son first got his place there. Arriving late she had missed some of the tour, but was not especially impressed with the building - 'it looked a bit like a prison'. But she liked the sound of what the school was trying to do, and the headmaster's approach seemed to value the children, not just aim to impress the parents. At the grammar school, on the other hand, she had been irritated to find that they were making an appeal for funds to preserve a historic part of the building which was only used for adult functions. 'What use is that to the children? They'd do better to work for a swimming pool!'

Whether at comprehensive or grammar school, the main thing was for the teacher to contrive to get the best out of the child. This was the really important educational relationship.

At home, the children certainly did not have it all their own way. They had to toe the line, and a cane across the knees might help the boys to do so. 'My fourteen-year-old thinks it's terrible but he has to put up with it - they don't get too cheeky! But I don't think girls should be walloped.'

Thinking about her daughters' future, Mrs. Morgan hoped that they would 'take up something they could go back to. I've always wished I'd gone in for typing or something so that when you've had a family you can go back and get a little job, something that fits in with the family and doesn't interfere too much. A friend of mine does office work for a few weeks at a time - I think that's a good idea.'

Mrs. Morgan was hard up, not in the best of health, and

had received little formal education. She was far from being an apathetic parent but she was likely to prove an invisible one, so far as the secondary school was concerned, unless something went seriously wrong for the children. She had decided views about discipline, formal education and the shape of her own maternal role. It is only through her children that her influence will extend beyond her local authority backwater.

Interview with Mr. Jackson

Mr. Jackson was a tall slim policeman in his mid-thirties. His tall slim wife was dressmaking in the background as he talked to the interviewer in the living room of their tidy council house. The time was mid afternoon but Mr. Jackson had only just got up, as he was on night duty. Mrs. Jackson joined in the discussion from time to time, but when the two children came in from school she got them a meal in the kitchen and kept them out of the way, while their father continued to debate educational matters with evident enjoyment.

The impression was of a husband and wife team working in considerable harmony, for whom 'the children' ranking with each other as members of the next generation, but whose individual characteristics did not pass unnoticed.

For Mr. Jackson, to talk about school was to talk about learning, rather than about relationships. The Jackson's children both attended the same comprehensive school, where their daughter was in fourth year and their son in second year. A lot of thought had gone into the choice of secondary school when the first child moved on from primary school, but then their son had followed his sister to the same school for the convenience of his parents.

The school was thought to be doing quite a good job, and was being left to get on with it. 'Only where it is absolutely necessary should you have direct contact with the school. It disrupts the school if you keep running up there.' Nevertheless, as the Jacksons often told their children 'if you do run into a problem it's no good hoping it's going to go away. You've got to do something about it.' In line with this belief, husband and wife had repeatedly gone to the primary school during the boy's early years, until they had finally convinced the headteacher that their son could not read and were allowed to take books to help him at home.

The primary school years, Mr. Jackson considered, were the crucial period during which the teacher must bring the child's mind to a 'readiness to learn'. Progressive styles of teaching were experimental, and his son and other children had lost ground by being the unwitting subjects of an experiment. Parents should certainly intervene and even make a nuisance of themselves if the school was not doing its job effectively.

The children were now both getting on well at school, so

the Jacksons were rarely seen there. Mr. Jackson had no taste for school entertainments, and did not propose to spend his time off doing things he did not enjoy. He and his wife kept fairly well informed about what was going on at school by questioning their children, and they took the opportunity to question the interviewer on her own views about the standard of the school's work and discipline.

Keeping an eye on homework was another way in which the Jacksons kept in touch with their children's secondary schooling. Mr. Jackson was critical of the 'fits and starts' pattern of some subject teaching, and its apparent lack of logical sequence. The wide range of subjects, and the integration of some subject disciplines, also made it rather difficult to get an overall view of what the children were learning. But by studying the children's textbooks he could get a grasp of the way they were supposed to be tackling the problems, and would try to help them in sorting this out without doing the work for them. He and his wife recognised that while both children might get the same out of school, what they put into their school work varied considerably. 'The girl will put all she can into it, but for the boy, if a page will do a page is what they get.'

Mr. Jackson was well aware that the range and nature of his police work coloured his outlook on life. He tried to maintain a tolerance of a wide range of behaviour, as long as it did not harm other people. There was, he felt, a greater willingness in society to show acceptance to those who did not conform to the usual pattern, and he was prepared to go along with this. But it made individual self discipline all the more necessary, and this was what he and his wife hoped to encourage in their children as they grew up.

Mr. Jackson had a wide experience of human behaviour, was conceptual in his thinking and seemed solidly educated in the form tradition. He and his wife were consciously working as educationally supportive parents, in a privatised way invisible to the school. They were interested in but not absorbed by their children, and gave the impression of maintaining a satisfying life of their own.

<u>Interview with Mrs. Berry</u>
It had taken some time to track Mrs. Berry down since she worked shifts at the airport. But she was pleased to have been approached. She had strong views about education and the parents' role and was clearly keen to put these across to the researcher.

Mrs. Berry and her only daughter, Lorraine, lived in a pleasantly furnished council maisonette, which reflected the neat feminine tastes of its occupants. The main room was light and airy with a striking number of books on the shelves beside the mantelpiece. In fact the interview took place on mother and daughter's return from the local library. Lorraine

A new enquiry

sat in on the interview with her mother.

Mrs. Berry immediately explained that she was an unmarried mother. It became clear that this was a central piece of information in understanding her attitude to education and to family life since she felt she had to be both mother and father to her child. She was determined that her daughter should not be disadvantaged and her attitude to school and her actions revolved around getting the best for Lorraine.

Mother and daughter obviously had a close and affectionate relationship, and were relaxed in each others company. An important component of their relationship was constructed around the daughter's school life and the interest her mother took in what was going on at school. Of all the parents encountered in the research, Mrs. Berry seemed to have the clearest idea of the content of school lessons and the educational process, and had clearly formed views about the adequacy and defects of these. She felt the best contribution she could make to her daughter's well-being was a sound and happy education. 'I can't leave her anything, so I've got to make sure she gets an education and can make her own way in life.'

Yet Mrs. Berry was highly aware of the danger of pushing Lorraine too hard and of projecting her own ambitions onto her daughter. In describing what she admitted as being her rather pushy and critical behaviour at primary school, especially over the choice of secondary school, she reflected that she had perhaps been aiming too high. Whilst it was a disappointment that Lorraine did not go to a single-sex grammar school, Mrs. Berry confessed that she had come to appreciate that Lorraine could be more comfortable in a school with slightly lower educational standards. In hoping that her daughter would learn from her mother's mistakes she had to be careful not to try to live her own life again through Lorraine. Although now she had a reasonably well paid job, Mrs. Berry felt she had failed to capitalise on her own educational opportunities. She had been to co-educational grammar school in the borough and remembered her schooldays as among the happiest in her life. She wanted Lorraine to be as happy but also to make more constructive use of her education.

It was evident that here was a mother with drive, determination and a thoughtful approach to the problem of her own situation. This carried through to her negotiations with the school. For example, one early problem was what to tell the school about Lorraine's background. Mrs. Berry wanted the school to be able to take account of Lorraine's unusual circumstances yet at the same time not to run the risk of her daughter being victimised by teachers who would express their disapproval. She resolved the matter by speaking confidentially to a respected senior teacher and was gratified by his response, which was to offer to keep a fatherly eye on

Lorraine and ask her to take any problems to him.

Mrs. Berry also explained how lonely it could be as a single parent. She commented on how she, perhaps more than other mothers, appreciated the opportunity of talking to other adults concerned with her child as normally there would be no one with whom to share her worries and aspirations. Meetings with teachers and hearing from them about how well her daughter was coping were treasured events. 'One teacher was ecstatic about her and it made me feel really good.'

Mrs. Berry's approach to the secondary school was a mixture of the demanding and the deferential. Her inclination to fight for her child and her own self confidence had led her to be openly critical of certain arrangements such as the narrowing of opportunities at the stage of choosing optional subjects, since her principal concern was to make sure Lorraine had every opportunity. Yet she sometimes refrained from making special visits and saved complaints up until the parents' evening because 'I don't like to bother them, they are too busy.' Although the school had a right to know about home circumstances, she considered that 'you can't go boring on about your own problems'. Similarly, although her views on education were developed and strongly held, she accepted that sometimes the teachers' opposing viewpoint was the right one. 'I have argued about exams (the need to go for 'O' level rather than CSE), but they may be right. I feel things strongly.' Mrs. Berry thought the teachers should take parents' views into account, but they might be justified in pursuing their own alternative line.

Her educational philosophy included an obsession with equality of opportunity yet at the same time a gearing of the educational system to producing excellence. Whilst regretting the dropping of old standards and recognising that Lorraine's school did not have a uniformly high reputation with all parents, she claimed that she could not have chosen a better school for her daughter. 'I'm thrilled to bits with the school.' Despite several attempts to get involved, she had never 'got into' the PTA although she thought its work in getting the new school building extremely worthwhile and contrasted the secondary school PTA with the primary school one where parents 'only joined to get special treatment for their kids. All the children of PTA members got to grammar school.'

Mrs. Berry's life as a parent could not however be described as strongly 'school centred'. Not only was she at a distance from several types of school based activities for parents, but her preoccupation with making sure Lorraine grasped all available opportunities led her to stimulate and sustain her daughter's interest in non-school activities such as tennis and music. And, however important the school was, she believed a child would only take full advantage of it if the parent was providing the appropriate back up and support.

A new enquiry

'Children are a product of their background and it's the irresponsible parents who cause delinquency and violence.' Indeed, she felt one of the really important tasks of the school and for society was to publicise the impact parents have. Her own attitudes were testimony to this approach.

Interview with Mrs. Cheng

Mrs. Cheng agreed to an interview when the researcher pointed out the intention to speak to parents with different experiences of contact with the school. Initially she had had some reservations about taking part because she had very little to do with the children's school.

Mrs. Cheng was a quietly-spoken Burmese lady living with her husband and her two younger children (a son and a daughter) in a 1930s terraced house outside the borough where the school was located. The family had left Burma in 1971 owing to the troubles there, and had initially stayed with friends near the school. In their eagerness to place their children in a British school, and given the requirements for the children to be accepted by a school, they had taken the first places offered. When the family finally settled in an adjacent borough, the question arose of a change of school, but the children had found friends in the original school and had wanted to stay. The travelling this then involved did not disturb Mrs. Cheng - 'I think it's been an education in itself, they've become more independent.'

The interview with the headteacher to place the children was the first and last visit made to the school by the parents. This was a little unexpected in the light of the concern the parents showed for education and the parents' own educational achievements. (Mrs. Cheng had taught English and maths in Burma.) But it soon became clear that a certain distance between family and school was taken for granted. Mrs. Cheng's philosophy was that the school played its part, and the family *its* part, but so long as things were not seriously wrong, they could work in parallel without direct contact. Mrs. Cheng expressed the hope that what the school taught was consistent with the values of the home, although in such a way that the researcher was left with the impression that the school had not quite come up to her expectations here.

Teachers at the school who had obviously never met Mrs. Cheng might have been surprised at the amount of 'behind the scenes' support the family offered to back up the school's efforts. It would have been easy to suppose that the distancing of the parents was due to a culture gap, and that the parents were finding it difficult to relate to British education. Far from this being so the mother in particular was consciously reassessing what were for her traditional ways of behaviour, and she was quick to recognise that what had been appropriate for her eldest daughter (educated to a high standard in Burma) would not do for her youngest child. 'It's necessary to be more aggressive here to get on. I have to be more tolerant of their new ways, and try not to be so strict.' She ruefully conceded that friends had a great deal of influence, but she was anxious not to pose a conflict for her daughter between Burmese values and British ones. Hence, she still tried to uphold the Buddhist faith in the home and quietly maintained a fairly traditional way of life in the home, at the same time as encouraging her son and daughter to bring their British friends home to the house, and to make it possible for her daughter to fit in with friends by buying up-to-the-minute clothes. It was clear that the chief anxiety had been for the children to settle down quickly, and this meant adapting to a new culture, not fighting it. This included accepting without complaint the introduction into her living room of a space-consuming hi-fi set bought with her son's first earnings.

What she knew of the school was what her children had told her. She was extremely appreciative of the help of a teacher who had taught them English (the children had known no English before their arrival), but now they no longer spoke of him she thought this teacher had left. (In fact he still taught at the school to the researcher's knowledge.) Perhaps because of her teaching background, she felt her major contribution to be over homework. With a great deal of home based tuition, the daughter had achieved an 'A' in maths. Most of her efforts had been directed towards the daughter, who was more amenable to the parents' influence and more interested in school work.

The family took for granted that the children would be dependent on their parents for several years to come. Both son and daughter had continued into the sixth form without question, and it was recognised that even as young employees they would still need the support of the home.

Mrs. Cheng did not expect schooling would directly contribute towards job skills, and she believed strongly in childhood being a period of enjoyment and fun. She contrasted he own convent education unfavourably with the lifestyle her daughter was able to pursue. If the school were to be involved in careers guidance, however, she expected the advice they would provide to be sound, and here her experience had not been promising, since the school appeared to have underestimated both her children's potential, especially her daughter's numerical ability.

Despite this and a few other instances which had evoked mild, if respectful, criticism from the parents, the parents insisted on their children looking up to their teachers. The father from time to time made the children send cards or gifts of fruit to the teacher to mark their respect and devotion as pupils.

The only time Mrs. Cheng had been tempted to go to the

A new enquiry

school to meet the teachers was over her son's withdrawn behaviour. She wondered if the school could have an influence here and bring him out a little more, but then concluded her son was naturally quiet and that as there was no evidence that his school work was suffering there would be no point in discussing it with the teachers. She found the teachers' written assessments of her children in most cases remarkably similar to her own evaluation, and with this degree of harmony between the family and school there was no pressing reason to discuss matters in greater depth directly with teachers.

Generally the parental role was conceived of as a stable and stabilising force in the background, there to be called upon by the child, and indeed the young adult, when necessary. She was cheered by her children's independence, not because it relieved her of responsibilities she was keen to lose, but because it marked them out for achievement, happiness and success in the future. Even though children became open to new influences parents still had an obligation to provide subtle unpressured guidance. Mrs. Cheng's solution was to engage her children in conversation about Burma and about Buddhism whenever opportunities presented themselves, and to keep around her relatively modern British home small mementoes of traditional culture, in the form of exquisite scenes depicted in ivory.

Interview with Mr. Clegg

Mr. and Mrs. Clegg lived in a grey, pebble-dashed, mid-terrace council house typical of several streets in the area. Mr. Clegg worked shifts and the family were apparently in fairly modest circumstances. Their elder child, a son of twenty-six, still lived at home, and the daughter (the subject of the interview) was at the point of leaving school after a year in the lower sixth. They were not young parents, and cordially admitted their daughter regarded them as 'old fuddy-duddies'. The mother was born and brought up in the area, whilst the father still retained a strong Glaswegian accent.

Their daughter, in contrast with her brother, was academically very bright. She had passed the 11-plus examination, and at that time this had meant going to a single sex grammar school, although the parents would have preferred a coeducational school. It was evident that the child's success at this stage had left the parents feeling peripheral and without much influence. Arrangements appeared to be being made on their child's behalf with the minimum of consultation with the parents. They were summoned to the grammar school, in the parents' phrase 'to be looked over', and bombarded with questions about the home background. The father maintained that all along he wished his daughter had not gone there, but whatever pride they had taken in their child's achievement rapidly turned to disillusionment with the school. They claimed the school was only concerned with the top twenty per cent of its pupils, and their daughter became increasingly unhappy. Eventually, the question of a change was brought up, and the education office offered the possibility of the girl transferring to one of the comprehensive schools in our study.

The son had attended the same school whilst it was still a secondary modern and the parents' memories of the school were not happy. However, it soon became clear that the school had changed considerably since those days. Lengthy discussions with the school counsellor and other members of staff convinced the parents that transfer to the comprehensive school would be the best thing for their daughter.

For the Cleggs, the content of home/school relations was the child's progress, which meant they gave parents' evenings some priority but other school based events scarcely figured in discussions. Their stated reasons for attending parents' evenings were that the reports from the teachers were so laconic that they wanted to confront the teachers to find out what they really thought. They said that once they heard a fuller account from the teacher, various attributes of their daughter became more understandable. The researcher also got the impression that after the son's singularly unsuccessful experience of secondary school, the parents were anxious not to let things deteriorate by default on their part.

Yet the content of their contact with the comprehensive school did not prove entirely satisfactory. The daughter, obviously very competent and self-confident, coped sufficiently well to cause no further concern and in the time available for discussion with teachers it was not possible for the parents to probe and find out more about school subjects. The picture that emerged was one of the parents wishing to show interest and be involved, but where the achievements of the daughter took education matters well beyond the parents' own experience and understanding. They were therefore condemned to be at one remove from their daughter's education.

Not that the comprehensive school was difficult to approach, as the parents explained. Some of the remoteness from their daughter's education was undoubtedly influenced by the girl herself who did not like them to show too much interest. On certain occasions her mother had thought about going to talk over particular matters with the school, but had been dissuaded by her daughter. Fortunately, although Mr. and Mrs. Clegg felt they did not have enough information to participate as actively as they would have wished in offering guidance and in keeping track of school affairs, the daughter showed a willingness to be influenced for the good by the teachers, particularly the younger teachers. For this the parents were extremely thankful.

The interview was especially interesting for the contrasts the parents repeatedly drew between the old secondary modern school (poor, narrow and badly staffed), the remaining grammar schools (snobby, narrow and uncaring) and

A new enquiry

the new comprehensives (broad in range and, if a little on the large side, where at least the teachers tried to compensate by making sure the children did not become anonymous). As parents, they had had to come to terms with different aspects of the state education system, and from a restricted knowledge base, had done their best to ensure their children were happy and able to benefit from their education. From the difference in the aptitudes of their son and daughter, they concluded the education must be tailored to the individual, and here the comprehensive had succeeded more than the other types of school.

These five distilled accounts of interviews give some impression of the range of family circumstances and attitudes encountered in the research. We are grateful to all the 109 families who, out of their tolerance, their interest or their courtesy agreed to tell us about their experiences and sometimes their philosophies of life. In this book we attempt to bring their family life experience into the public domain.

An indication of chapter and content may be helpful to the reader.

Chapter Two completes the introductory section of the book by recapitulating the themes pursued by earlier writers on home/school relationships. The next section, chapters Three to Seven, sets out the parents' views as expressed in the home interviews. The reader whose chief interest is in the detail of family experience may wish to move directly to these chapters.

Chapter Three deals with the run-up to secondary schooling. It gives parents' comments about the impact of the primary school years on the child and the home, and goes on to examine parents' evaluations of the contributions made by the family, the primary school and the local authority to the process of choice of secondary school. It also chronicles parents' implicit and explicit expectations of what the secondary school has to offer.

Chapter Four gives a detailed account of the actual contacts which parents had with the four comprehensive schools in our study. It sets our the hopes which teachers expressed for the outcome of such contacts as well as the parents' experience.

Chapter Five and Six explore the parents' perception of their own role during the secondary school years, firstly in relation to their children (chapter Five) and secondly in response to the requirements of their children's secondary schools (chapter Six).

Chapter Seven discusses the parents' experiences of school-related agencies including the school health, education welfare and careers service.

In the concluding section of the book, chapter Eight reassesses the potential of present-day relationships between home and secondary school. Finally, an appendix gives a full account of the methods of our study, and as much detail as research confidentiality will allow about the families whose experience is chronicled in this book.

Chapter Two

THEMES IN THE STUDY OF HOME/SCHOOL RELATIONS

In educational circles there is probably more agreement about the value of good home/school relationships than about anything else. But to appreciate the present-day amalgam of ideas as to what constitutes a good relationship between home and school, it is necessary to look back about the need to involve parents in the education of their children.

The issue of improving home/school relationships moved into prominence in the late 1950s and 1960s, but the value of parents' interest in schooling had not been totally overlooked before then. More than a century earlier, the 1844 Report of the National Society had commented: 'Until the home cooperates with the school room, education cannot exercise its legitimate influence.'

As elementary education became widespread and, eventually, compulsory, attention focussed on meeting the material needs of children from families whose private poverty was now made public in the schoolroom. The provision of school meals, and the setting up of the school medical service, were both stimulated in part by the 1904 enquiry into the 'Physical Deterioration of the Working Classes' (Cd. 2175), with its accounts of starving children.

By the 1930s, the idea of school-based welfare which could, at a discreet distance, supplement the deficiencies of the home, was giving way to the idea of a more individualised working relationship between teachers and parents. During that decade the first home and school council was set up, associated with the creation of some of the first parent/teacher associations. The council's activities ceased with the onset of war, but in the postwar decade of the 1950s a number of factors combined to bring about a revival of interest in the relationship between home and school.

The upsurge of interest

Following the 1944 Education Act, a number of enquiries were put in hand about the extent to which the widening educational opportunities offered by the Act were being grasped. 'Early Leaving' (HMSO, 1954) demonstrated that despite the tripartite system, which was intended to ensure the identification of those suited to extended education, there were those, principally from the working class, who dropped out of secondary education before their time. In differing ways the Crowther Report (1960) and the Newsom Report (1963) highlighted similar problems.

These government enquiries into the pattern of take up of educational opportunities coincided with a growth in academic research into the relative influences of environment and innate ability on achievement. Successive studies highlighted that the child's environment was likely to play as great a part in affecting 'educability' as was inborn intelligence. (Floud et al, 1956; Nisbet, 1953; Fraser, 1959). Floud contended that 'with the expansion of educational opportunity and the reduction of ... economic handicaps to children's school performance, the need arises to understand the optimum conditions for the integration of school and home environment at all levels.'

During this period, the chief focus both of the committees of enquiry and the academic investigations was on waste of talent, through lack of development of the intellectual resources of the working class, and the loss for the nation which this wastage represented. It was claimed that 'social class plays an important part in determining the use that children admitted to the grammar schools can make of the course or, from the point of view of occupational structure, the extent to which they ... equip themselves for and enter the grade of occupation for which their abilities make them eligible.' (Halsey et al, 1961). A few years on, Blyth was making the same points. 'If we are concerned, as we must be, both with individual development and with the optimum use of the nation's resources and talents, then the means of stimulation or retardation (of the relationship between the home environment and the education process) must matter.' (Blyth, 1967)

In addition to developing the notion of home and school relationships, studies beginning in the 1950s also cast doubt on the validity of selection for different types of secondary education. One political outcome of the analysis of whether all pupils took advantage of the educational opportunities open to them was the conversion of many to the ideal of comprehensive education. In the 1950s and 1960s, the concern for home/school relationships and for the advancement of comprehensive schooling remained parallel interest.

Themes of home/school relations

Whilst the economic barriers to working class take-up of extended education had been discerned at an early stage, it had been supposed that an alleviation of these material difficulties, through appropriate support, would unfetter the working class child. When this was found not to be so, the answer was sought in the 'attitude' of the parents and the prevailing values of the community. The emphasis of investigation shifted from the study of material disabilities to the social factors which appeared to influence intellectual development. The new aim was 'to explore the social and cultural circumstances affecting attainment or performance at a given level of ability.' (Halsey et al, 1961)

Ensuing studies concluded that the relatively low value set on formal education, the lack of encouragement to study for its own sake and the parents' own low educational achievements all counteracted the school's educational influence on the working class child. The potential discomfort of the child, torn by conflicting values and expectations was not the least of the damaging effects of a lack of fit between home and school attitudes. One of the principal aims of those advocating the improvement in home/school relationships was the education of the parents, so as to harmonise the values of home and school to the point that the talented child was not inhibited from taking his studies further. Hence, the chief reason for teachers to contact parents was for parents to learn of the importance of education, and to come to agree with the school. The relationship, from the outset, was bound to be asymmetrical.

Further studies in the 1960s introduced new perspectives on the need for contact, but were still concerned with the difficulties the child faced when subjected to two opposing influences, and still assumed that one of the beneficial outcomes of parent/teacher contacts would be that the parent would come to understand the worth of education and subscribe to its values. The opinion held by researchers and educationists of at least a hardcore of working class parents was very low. Blyth (1967) identified a group of parents who were 'hostile' to education, and another group of 'passive nonconformists' characterised by 'low intelligence and an almost complete lack of organising ability'. These assessments were in the same vein as an earlier analysis by Davis (1950) which suggested that 'feckless' parents might learn foresight and moderation by mixing socially with parents from the middle class.

From a recognition that parents' attitudes mattered, literature on home/school relations moved on to indicate that the conversion of parents would be incomplete unless they understood *why* their view mattered, and hence why they should alter not only their attitudes but their behaviour. A number of studies attempted to explore the impact on children's education of different types of parenting. Wiseman (1964),

Douglas (1964) and Mays (1962) all concluded that the 'interest' shown by parents made a crucial difference to the progress of the child. Douglas' study was the most detailed in the analysis of this interest and its impact. From the outset, teachers have tended to equate parental interest with physical attendance at school events, and this view was still put forward by teachers participating in our own research. It will be part of our thesis to suggest that there are many other forms of interest in the child which must be taken into account before dismissing parents as apathetic or unconcerned with their child's education.

To a limited degree, Douglas too tried to extend the definition of an 'interested parent' through he still relied heavily on teachers' reports. The parent deemed to be showing high interest was both a regular attender of school events and was rated by the teacher as giving support in the home, by reading, playing and providing stimulus for the child. His study found that significant advances in attainment correlated with 'high parental interest', and relative decline in attainment with 'low interest'. Douglas was scrupulous in trying to avoid the kind of teacher rating bias towards the middle class which different parts of the same study revealed over the question of streaming. A finding of implicit significance was that the attainment of middle class pupils whose parents did not show interest (who in effect did not visit the school) nonetheless did not suffer so much as the attainment of working class pupils whose parents also appeared to be uninterested. This was explained with reference to the higher education aspirations in the neighbouring middle class families and amongst the friends of these pupils, or the relatively high academic standards at the primary schools they attended. But the fact that interest could be communicated to children without parents actually attending the school was not openly discussed. Whatever the flaws of Douglas' study, it made its points persuasively and well, and partly because of it, the need to stimulate parent interest became established as a central objective of parent/teacher relationships.

Mays' study (1962) introduced another nuance into home/school relationships - the need to comprehend the environment of the child. Until now, the learning role in any encounter between teacher and parent fell to the parent. With Mays' study came the appreciation that home/school contact could instruct and help the teacher. It revealed a widespread ignorance among teachers about the home lives of their pupils.

One of Mays' recommendations was for teachers to undertake more home visiting, and not simply to lament the lack of parental support for the school. Whilst one of the desired outcomes was again the promotion of interest amongst parents, and showing them how they could help the school, Mays appreciated that even if this did not always occur, the teacher would have gained insight and tolerance through contact with parents. He also pointed to the obligation of teachers themselves to facilitate good relationships. 'Parental apathy is frequently commented on by teachers when questioned about their work in downtown schools, and the many problems associated with their work. Many of the teachers are critical of the parents and consider them to be failing in their duties. There is little doubt ... that an over-censorious attitude on the part of teachers, where it exists, must make relationships between home and school more difficult than they might otherwise be.'

It should not of course be assumed that until this time teachers were unaware of the need to get to know their pupils' circumstances, but for the kind of cases Mays was discussing, it had more often been left to the old 'school board man' to come to terms with the family's home environment, and act as an intermediary between home and school. The need for teachers to come to grips with the families at first hand was a new idea.

CONTACTING PARENTS

By the mid-sixties, parent/teacher contact was firmly on the agenda for development, and the question of mechanisms of contact was more at issue than whether contact was a good thing. The most common response of schools was to rely on and develop institutional contacts, notably the open evening or parents' evening, and, though less frequently, the parent/teacher association.

The practice of holding parents' evenings was already fairly well established as part of the reporting procedure of many schools. These evenings now came to be seen as a potentially important linkage between parent and teacher. Firmly based on the undoubted interest of the parent in his or her own child, the event provided an opportunity for the teacher to familiarise parents with the school's objectives for the child's education, and how the parent could contribute to these.

Parents' evenings are still a prominent element in the arrangements for home/school contact which prevail in most secondary schools today although, as our own research illustrates, the expectations which parents bring to such events are not always in line with those of the teachers.

So far as parent/teacher associations are concerned, these have had a more chequered history. Their scattered incidence in schools today, the patchy support which they evoke, and the existence in some schools of parents' associations or 'friends of the school', with apparently less equivocal terms of reference than the fullblown PTA, are testimony to uncertainties of aim and scope which were demonstrated when the movement began.

From the outset, many teachers stated their opposition to PTAs on the grounds that they would appeal only to parents the school already had no difficulty in contacting. A countervailing argument was that of using the parents already identified as 'interested' as an important platform from which to move to attract those as yet less involved. Another argument was that a parent/teacher association, in principle, allowed the meeting of the two parties on a more equal footing than many other school based events. Furthermore, the relative formality of such an association might be seen as providing a model of calm and order to be adhered to in less formalised ad hoc encounters between parents and teachers. The irate parent interrupting the lesson was not the picture which schools wished to evoke in making sure there were more opportunities for parents and teachers to meet.

Of course, the pressure to set up PTAs came in many cases not from the school but from certain parents. The prospect of intensified home/school relationships in the form of a parent teacher association was not immediately welcomed by or appealing to many headteachers and their staff. Nevertheless the trend was by now inexorably towards greater contact, impelled not only by the established findings of research but by increasingly vociferous pressure groups such as the Campaign for the Advancement of State Education (CASE), the Advisory Centre for Education (ACE) and the revived Home and School Council. While much of the pressure towards increased parent teacher contact was a response to the realisation of the limited take up of educational opportunity, and the investigations into this phenomenon, another outcome, as noted above, had been increased interest in comprehensive schools. Some of the groups most interested in exerting pressure to end selection and streaming were concerned and articulate parents. As these parents saw comprehensive education getting under way, some of their energies were released into their associated concern, the say of parents in the education of their children.

The Plowden Report 'Children and Their Primary Schools' coming in 1967 provided a big fillip to parent/teacher movements and laid great stress on the value of parent/teacher relationships. But although it had enormous impact and consolidated the trend towards home/school relationships (and imparted to the assessment of those relationships the primary school ambiance which has proved so pervasive and enduring), the report conveys a sense of prior commitment towards partnership rather than advocacy based on the findings of the large amount of research which the Committee commissioned.

The report was nevertheless at least in part the stimulus for several new studies of the way parents should be involved in schooling. All kinds of suggestions for interaction between parents and schools began to be offered. Accounts of good practice were published by the Department of Education

Themes of home/school relations

and Science in 'Parent/Teacher Relations in Primary Schools' (1968), and the promulgation of good practice was also accomplished through such enthusiastic accounts of innovation as McGeeney's 'Parents are Welcome' (1969). A report to the DES, 'Teachers and Parents' (Report No. 41, 1967) identified informal contact between parents and teachers as less artificial than 'on show' events, and to be encouraged.

The need to establish contact with parents who did not regularly attend school events was tackled in a number of ways. ACE was instrumental in setting up, on an experimental basis, education shops, where parents could drop in and find out more about education in general and about schools. From these experiments, it was concluded that many parents were starved of information, and would be happy to have more opportunities of finding out about their children's education.

At about this time there was also an upsurge of interest in 'community schools'. Again this was not a novel idea, and had its origins in the thirties with the village colleges of Cambridgeshire. But the emphasis on creating a natural and welcoming environment in the school persuaded many that the way forward was to make sure the school opened up resources to parents, and became a focal point of the community. A not inconsiderable advantage of community schooling was held to be that, as natural centres for continued education, these schools could also get at and educate parents who would not normally participate in further education. The enthusiastic adoption of community schooling in educationally disadvantaged areas (Midwinter, 1973) shows their popularity as tools for environmental change and as positive instruments to go out and reach people remote from education. This is somewhat in contrast to the assumptions of the earliest village colleges that they would represent a natural outgrowth of existing local interest, although the imposition of high culture which accompanied the earliest colleges suggests that even that ideal was circumvented from the start. Both during the 1930s and in more recent manifestations, community schools have been appraised not just as a facility to be called upon by an interested local population, but as means of changing that population and as a counter to possibly anti-educational features in the local community.

Home visiting by teachers, one technique, widely reported to be effective in establishing contact with families not normally seen at the school and advocated back in 1964 by Mays, was then and has since been consistently under-utilised. Instead, an increasing number of other professionals and agency workers have been called on to act as intermediary between home and school. The early theme of welfare as an important enabler of cooperation between home and school has had a recrudescence. In its new form, concern has extended beyond the material problems of families to their possible psychological problems. A whole welfare network now exists to which the schools have licensed if disjointed access, and a number of workers are engaged not only in their own specialised tasks but in the role of intermediary between home and school, or home and agency, or agency and school. Educational psychologists, education welfare officers, school counsellors and school based social workers are all examples here. In the literature on home/school relations this growth of the intermediary role has been chronicled in successive editions of 'Linking Home and School' (1967, 1972, 1980) and discussed as a concept by Fitzherbert (1977) and Robinson (1979). But, with the exception of the rare specialised home/school liaison teacher, the part played by the ordinary teacher in home/school relationships has not expanded beyond the confines of school premises.

The majority of contacts established and experimented with by teachers during the 1970s and up to the present day have been on school premises and on the teachers' terms. Schools' successes in managing home/school relationships are still measured against the yardstick of having parents 'up' to the school, and as we saw earlier, the parents presence at school is widely assumed to be the same as the parents' interest in the child's education.

ACCOUNTABILITY AND PARTICIPATION

Relating to parents in the teachers' own terms was a luxury which many teachers began to feel would be denied them as another and quite distinct trend of home/school relationships developed in the late sixties and early seventies - that of parental participation in the running of the school, and parents' right to know what was happening in the school. Until this time the parent/teacher relationship was asymmetrical, with the teacher holding very nearly a monopoly of information and control. The prevailing trend towards participation apparent in other educational establishments, in public affairs and in private industry was chiefly articulated in relationship to schools by the already formed pressure groups such as CASE and through some parent/teacher associations. Its principal manifestation was a demand for parental representation on the board of governors, but this was accompanied by pressure for more open schools, community schooling, use of school resources outside school hours and the accountability of teachers to their clients, both parents and pupils.

The source of the pressure caused many teachers to dismiss this as 'middle class manipulation' and to question its validity. Yet the reality of the trend towards participation could readily be seen within the teaching profession itself. Alongside the claims of parents for involvement with the school there was evidence of equal if not overriding concern within some schools about the way in which teachers' own views and aspirations for education could be represented.

The idea of parents becoming governors was not entirely new. Deliberation prior to the drafting of the Education Act in 1944 had included consideration of whether a parent governor should be appointed to the governing body of schools. The 1944 Act also recognised the legitimate say of parents in the schooling of their children, at least in connection with religious education, language, medical facilities and coeducation. Yet the story usually became one of campaigns fought by well organised pressure groups of parents in individual local authorities for the acceptance of the notion of parental participation, although there were some authorities and schools which much more readily accepted the view that parents should be involved in the management of schools. By the time our study took place, it was not uncommon for there to be a representative of the parents on the governing body of secondary schools, but the two boroughs involved in the research had only just embarked upon these innovations.

The parents' rights as consumers were being advocated in a different way in party political circles. The parents' right to exercise choice of schooling was taken up by the Conservative Party, and a number of ideas floated, such as voucher systems, open publication of schools' examination results and so on. These matters are still under debate, but they reflect a new emphasis on the parent as a client with a right to know about the schools. This can legitimately be seen as part of the same kind of trend towards accountability as parental participation in decision making in schools. Nevertheless the assumptions and desired outcomes are rather different in spirit from those underlying the pressure to have parents more actively engaged in the management of schools.

Of the two approaches to making the education system more accountable to its clients, the one that showed signed of taking off in the seventies was the participation of parents in the management of state schools. The Taylor Committee reported in 1977 on reform of the government of schools (HMSO, 1977) and one of its central premises was that there were four groups that should have equal representation on a school's governing body. These were the local education authority, the staff, parents and pupils (one single category) and the local community. The powers that the Taylor Committee recommended be delegated to a school's governing body meant that more than simply lip-service was being paid to the importance of parents. The report was an explicit statement of the desirability of a more equal partnership between parents and teachers, and of confidence in the benefits which a thorough involvement of parents would bring to the school and the individual child. Subsequent developments in the potential for home/school relations, brought about by the 1980 Education Act and its attendant political debate cannot be appraised here, but will be briefly reflected on in our final chapter.

Despite the fact that our research took place during the period of maximum publicity for the Taylor Report's proposals, the level of consciousness among parents about their potential role in decision making at the four schools remained low. For the majority of parents and teachers in our study, the raison d'etre of home/school relationships was not associated with increased accountability, but with the issues raised earlier – getting to know the pupils' environment, learning about what the school stood for and coordinating the influences on the child.

Ideas which are at the forefront of educationalists' interest nevertheless take some time to work their way through to the practice of schools and local authorities. We therefore turn to the account of parents' perspectives on their children's secondary schooling in the late 1970s, with confidence that they retain much relevance for teachers and parents negotiating a home/school relationship in the 1980s.

Part II

The new research

Chapter Three

BEFORE THE SECONDARY SCHOOL YEARS

The focus of our study is the relationship between family and school during the secondary school years. But both parents and pupils approach the secondary school with expectations and attitudes influenced by the child's years in primary school, and also by the years at home which precede all school experience. The home life of their pupils, which secondary school teachers hope will favourably influence the child's progress and his attitude to education, has been developing and changing for more than a decade by the time the new entrant arrives in the secondary school. In this chapter we therefore draw on those of our research data which refer to stages in family experience which precede the secondary school years.

STARTING SCHOOL

Both for parents and child a moment of transition comes when the child has to go to school. He and his parents stand at the beginning of at least eleven years' compulsory involvement with the education system. If the parents have more than one child, or if the child himself stays at school beyond the minimum school leaving age, that involvement will be much longer, and may constitute the family's most sustained and consistent contact with a public institution throughout the years the family remains together.

As parents set about getting their child started at primary school they assume new public responsibilities, and share or relinquish some private ones. The onus is squarely on the parents to get the child to school, whether he be eager, phlegmatic or upset, and the parent who takes the eldest child in the family to school for the first time is taking on a new public dimension of the parental role. In families we talked with, it had usually been the mother who took on this role. Most people can remember their own first day at school. Mothers tend to remember their children's first days as well, and the ensuing days too, when children are eager to go again or perhaps taken aback to find that going to school is not a once-for-all experience but a new dimension of daily life. Only the first child in the family to go to school is likely to be surprised to find that he has to go again, but parents did not always find that getting younger children started at school was easier because older brothers and sisters were going as well. The eldest, the middle ones, or the last child at home were equally likely to be identified as the most reluctant starters, and for many parents the physical handing over and leaving of their children was a laborious and regularly re-negotiated process which they found physically and emotionally wearing.

For some mothers the same experience was repeated as each son or daughter started school, but often some children in the family would settle in immediately, even discouraging parents from seeing them part of the way to school. It was not always these children who were still liking school when we encountered their families several years later, nor did those who had got off to a troubled start necessarily dislike school later on. But parents remembered these first beginnings, and their own strategy towards their children's school experience was sometimes that of a phased withdrawal which they thought it inappropriate to reverse when the child became a secondary school pupil.

The process by which parents gradually drew back from their child's side at school was initially a physical one. A kind of weaning from protection and escort was taking place, the stages in which were normally planned by the parent, but sometimes hastened by an initiative from the child. One mother said: "I always take them, all the time they're at primary school. It eases my mind to know they are there within the gates. I see the smallest one right into the classroom, as a rule." In another family the children were taken only for the first week: "The boy in particular didn't want us to take him after that." Some children were particularly reluctant starters: "I had to drag my daughter up there every day for a month, when she first started. But now she loves it."

But whatever the experiences of those earlier days, the move from home to infant school inevitably involved parent as well as child, in a way that subsequent changes of school would not necessarily do.

EARLY HOME/SCHOOL RELATIONSHIPS

Some parents saw the whole purpose of parental involvement with the primary school as being 'for the child', that is for his personal development and emotional security, rather than 'for his education', that is for skills he might acquire or the learning progress he might make, at school. These parents felt it appropriate to continue weaning the child not only from their escort and surveillance to and from school, but also to some extent from their involvement and participation in school activities. One mother commented: "You have more to do with the infants - it gives them a good start, especially when they are very small. When they are going up to the juniors, drop off a bit. But when they are small, they need Mum about. As they get older, they want to stand on their own feet, not have Mum always behind them - she can take an interest but not tie them to her apron strings. They know she has taken an interest, when they were small."

For parents who take this view, one of the main motivations for parental involvement in the child's school life may no longer be operational, by the time the child gets to secondary school. They consider he no longer requires their physical protection or emotional support - and if he *does* seem to want it, parents may feel uneasily that he has taken a step backward in his development. Parental motivation to take an interest in their children's secondary school life is, in this respect as in some others, likely to be different from that which drew them to the primary school.

It was evident from the recollections of most of the families we encountered that their children's primary schools had been essentially local institutions. Few children travelled far to their primary school, and it the family moved house during the primary years, even though still within the same general area, children were usually transferred to a school close by. If parents took their children to primary school they were likely to see other parents and children from the immediate district whom they already knew or at least recognised. This meant that the new 'public' role of the parent of a school-child was played out before acquaintances rather than strangers. Depending on the relationships between families in the area, this might be seen as an advantage or a disadvantage. For some parents, the eventual transfer to secondary school gave them an opportunity they had long been waiting for, to find the child a part-time environment out of the immediate neighbourhood, away from well-known local families and groups of friends.

A change of primary school could often bring about a marked change in the level of home/school contact, in which the most influential variable seemed to be the line taken by the school about parental involvement. None of the parents interviewed appeared to have been kept outside the school gate, or deterred from taking a reluctant school-attender right into the classroom, but some schools did not limit the parent's role to that of escort. They might be encouraged to help the teachers, perhaps by turning out cupboards, or hearing children read, or helping with arrangements for special events. One mother commented that at Christmas time she was more in the primary school than in her own home.

The same mother found that when the children went to another primary school, following a house move, her assistance was still welcomed, but at the more formal level of a supplementary escort on school trips. At this school, she had the impression that parental participation was not encouraged as a matter of principle, but that selected parents were invited to help. "I think they pick their parents. There are a few very unruly children. *Their* parents might not be good to come in." The views held by these parents, she implied, might upset the running of the school. However, we cannot assume, as this parent appeared to, that all parents are equally eager to play an active part in their children's primary school. The variation in the extent to which parents see their children's primary school - or indeed their secondary school - as a penetrable institution is a function not only of the school's attitude but also of the parent's disposition and desires.

Whether or not the family moves house during the child's primary school years, the transfer between infant and junior school means that by the age of eleven most children have already been to two schools, and often their experience in each has been distinctly different. A number of parents we encountered distinguished between the infant and the junior schools their children had attended as two disjunctive experiences rather than one amorphous 'primary' whole to be contrasted en bloc with the secondary school. Most frequently they attributed the difference to the style and influence of the headteacher.

Remarks which parents made about their children's primary school - whether 'infants' or 'junior' - indicated that they perceived both the school's organisational structure and its style as being capable of being influenced or controlled by one person. The headteacher was frequently referred to as 'running' the school - a phrase much less frequently used in connection with secondary school headteachers.

Primary school class teachers, although perceived as conforming to an overall school policy, were often well-known individuals recognised by parents as making distinctive contributions to the children's school life. One mother commented that there were only four teachers at the primary school, and she had got to know them all quite well, with the result that she felt 'a lot more comfortable' there than at the secondary school. Another parent said she knew all the primary school teachers as individuals and would recognise them passing by. More primary school than secondary school teachers, it seemed, lived in the area where they worked. If, with the passage of time, they had moved on to other schools, parents often knew what local schools they now worked in, and what promotion they had obtained.

For most parents the smaller size and simpler

organisational structure made it easier to get a grasp of the school 'set-up' at the primary stage. The small number of teachers meant a more manageable range of encounters, when parents visited the school. Yet there were some disadvantages to the smaller size and more intimate atmosphere of the primary school. If one known and trusted teacher left, out of half a dozen, her loss was more important. And if teacher and child did not get on well together, the 'cosiness' of the small school might become claustrophobic.

For one family, whose daughter was by now in her third year at secondary school, the memory of a conflict with the infants school was still vivid. A difficulty about the child eating up her school dinners had, in the father's view, developed into a personality clash between the headmistress and the child which became an obsession on the headteacher's part. She took over personal supervision of the child's meals; the resulting 'scenes' were reported to the mother by the dinner ladies. The parents got their general practitioner to write to the headmistress, who then wrote to the parents asking them to remove their child from the school. The mother refused, then got a letter from the local education authority asking the same, since the child was 'not eating her meals'. After the parents had talked the matter over with an education officer, the dispute died down and the child was allowed to finish her time at the school. Years later, however, the parents still cited the episode as a serious setback to the development of their timid daughter's self confidence.

Another mother, whose daughter in the infants school thoroughly disliked the teacher, recognised that the teacher in turn disliked her daughter. With a brisk use of psychology, mother got daughter to take teacher a present - and things improved.

These are examples of the personal and intimate teacher/pupil relationships which the small school may engender, in which parents may sometimes feel called upon to intervene. However, it was more characteristic for the parent/teacher relationship to be a direct one, from which the child's youth and vulnerability set him a little apart. Parents and teachers could encounter one another 'over his head' - a situation which would be familiar to him from his parents' meetings with other adults. This was a time at which many parents felt most on a level with teachers. They might be near to one another in age; certainly nearer than either was to the child, whereas secondary school teachers were often perceived by parents as closer in age to their senior pupils than to the parents.

The custodial role of the primary school teacher towards the child was still an important one, as it was for the parents. The teacher could readily appreciate the need to keep a special check on the whereabouts of a small child, on days when he was likely to run home because he knew his mother

Before secondary school

was going shopping.

Teachers and parents found it appropriate to be in close touch with one another about the child's health during the more vulnerable years of early childhood. Parents could, and did, tell the teachers about children's nightmares, tummy-aches, earache or spots without feeling they were being over-protective. Teachers too found it appropriate to approach parents about their concern over children's health. One mother recalled that it was at the repeated urging of the infants school headteacher that she had taken her son to the paediatrician who diagnosed his muscular dystrophy. By the time secondary school is reached, serious defects have usually been noted and most minor and childish ailments are in the past, so that a mutual concern about the child's ill health is more rarely a point of contact between parent and teacher.

Very occasionally, the directness and friendly quality of the relationship between teacher and parent seemed to mean that the child's best interests were no longer the first consideration. One father, worried about his son's possible backwardness, thought teachers might be trying to cheer him up, in assuring him all was well: "Are they telling me the truth or are they bolstering me up? They say he's progressing slightly, but we don't see much of it here. I wonder if I ought to see a doctor or psychiatrist about him."

While the vulnerability of the child's age group and the shared concern for his physical and emotional wellbeing provided a potential bond between parent and teacher, it was another aspect of the age group, and the protective feelings it evoked, which contributed to a parental experience of the primary school which would not be repeated at the secondary school stage. This was the pleasure experienced in watching young children - one's own and those of other parents - in their early attempts at mutual cooperation and display. While parents were often admiring of the calibre of dramatic presentations or sporting events put on at secondary school, their children's participation in these events did not evoke the same emotions as at the primary school stage. Several mothers spontaneously recalled their pleasure in these events. "I used to love watching the sports at (junior school)." "I went to every play they did. Once my son was a choir boy angel." "The concert in the infants was ever so good, and the plays in the juniors. I like to see all that."

Another factor which helped parent keep in touch with their children's life at primary school was the relatively elementary nature of their school work. The bafflement which many parents were to feel about the titles and the content of subjects taught in the secondary school had not yet intervened to distance the parent from the child's school experience. Whatever the teaching methods and teaching aids used in the primary school, the substance of what children learnt at this time was comprehensible and familiar to parents. And the primary schoolteacher's expertise was not so specialised as to overawe parents whose own education had been brief. These teachers were doing an understandable, even a homely job of imparting basic educational skills. In some cases, parents felt they could with confidence be critical of what the teachers achieved, especially so far as children's progress in reading was concerned.

Whether or not children were seen as having had particular educational problems during the primary school years, the final year at junior school seemed very frequently to have been the occasion of a conscious assessment of children by parents. The imminent transfer from primary to secondary education is as important a watershed in the child's life as when he first goes to school. We turn shortly to a discussion of parents' experience of this time of transfer.

In reflecting on these family experiences of the primary school years, it should not be concluded that these years are always a halcyon period of close relationships between home and school, followed by more stormy years of association with the secondary school. Parental accounts bore evidence to wide variations between particular primary schools' attitudes to home/school contacts. For some parents the secondary school was to prove infinitely more open, to others infinitely more closed.

As the children moved on to the comprehensive schools, they and their families already had experience of what a home/school relationship might be. It was on this experience that the secondary schools had to build.

CHOICE OF AND TRANSITION TO SECONDARY SCHOOL

The reorganisation of secondary school education on comprehensive lines was a relatively recent phenomenon in the boroughs where we conducted our research. Many parents had had children transfer from primary to secondary school both during a selective and a non-selective phase of educational provision. In the case of older children, who had reached a secondary school age at a time when selective schools were still admitting pupils, the advice of the primary school headteacher had been an important factor in the parents' named choice of school. In several cases a child's suitability for a grammar school education had been represented to the parents as 'borderline'. In most of these cases, parents had been unwilling to see their child under academic pressure and had felt he would be happier in a non-selective school where he was unlikely to be 'at the bottom of the pile". Lengthy secondary education was an unfamiliar experience in the areas where we made our study, and facing the implications of a grammar school placement could be a daunting prospect for the family. Several parents commented on the requirement to

Before secondary school

undertake that the child would be allowed to stay at grammar school for seven years.

Primary school headteachers' recommendations that a grammar school be named as first choice for an able child had not always been tactfully broached with parents. For one father, the recounting of his clash with his younger son's primary school headteacher was an appropriate and dramatic starting point for the discussion of his children's secondary schooling. The headteacher said the boy was capable of doing well, could get to a grammar school and might not complete his education until the age of 20 or even 25. The idea that going to grammar school might subsequently entail formal education to the age of 25 was anathema to the father, a successful self-employed man who put a high value on experience of work and life. He said to the headmaster that he himself left school at fifteen, was grown up by twenty and saving as well. In his view, someone emerging from the education system at 25 might be quite inexperienced, while someone who at nineteen had two years of experience of work and life after leaving school at seventeen would be superior to the 25 year old in his experience of the world. Feelings evidently continued to mount as the headteacher went on to ask the father how he would define happiness. He thought about it and then said "Money" (as long as in good health). "Rubbish", said the headmaster. "Well, there may be a few poor people who are happy, but I know a jolly sight more well off ones who are happy!" replied the father.

This had been a classic case of advice being given by a headteacher, couched in terms which the father was unable to accept. With hindsight, the father explained in interview that he had wanted to convey that he did not entirely agree with extended formal education to the exclusion of work experience. He was a firm believer in individual effort and achievement and felt that the individual had to take the chance that might come to him only once. He had not liked school himself. He had wanted to get to work and always knew he could make his way. Several of his friends had limited education, but were doing well with their own businesses. Getting on, he said, was a question of attitude. Nevertheless, he would have been quite happy for his son to go to grammar school as well as the local secondary modern school, which their elder son already attended, on the 'choice' form. However, they were not surprised that the boy did not in the end get a place a grammar school.

Few of the transfer decisions appear to have been made in such an emotionally charged atmosphere. Nevertheless, for most parents the move from the primary school was seen as some kind of turning point in the child's life. In moving on to examine in greater depth the factors influencing choice recounted by other parents, we have to recognise that the process of choice often harks back to a stage much earlier than the point at which the child under discussion moved from primary to secondary school. For very many families the choice of secondary school is made only once, when the first and eldest child leaves primary school. We shall return to this characteristic later in our discussion. Even more remotely, parents' own secondary school experience foreshadows and influences their wishes for their child.

Many of the parents we interviewed in these outer London boroughs had gone to the same school as their children now attended. At that time it had been a secondary modern school, often for girls or boys only. Parents commented at length on the changes of size, style, curriculum, discipline and amenities which had taken place, and yet some sense of familiarity and continuity seemed to colour their choice of the same school for their children. Sometimes it was the children themselves who elected to go there, even if the school was at some little distance from the parental home. One mother, whose son had firmly opted to go out of their present neighbourhood to the school she herself had once attended, commented that his choice may have been influenced by the tales she had told him about her time at school, or perhaps by the fact that her own mother, still living nearby, would give her grandson lunch. These factors of family organisation and convenience are another point to which we will return.

In making the choice of secondary school, there are parents who put the child and his characteristics at the centre, and others who give first consideration to the perceived characteristics of the school. The great majority of parents had consulted their child and taken some account of his wishes in naming their choice of secondary school. In a number of families, the choice had been unequivocally the child's. Parents often related this abnegation of their own role in the decision to the importance of the child's attitude towards his future school. It was seen as crucial to all his future schooling that he should want to go to that particular school at that particular time in his life. And it was freely recognised that his wish to go there was usually dependent on the fact that his friends were likely to go to the same school. Given that younger brothers and sisters are likely to follow the eldest child to his preferred secondary school, the influence of these first young friends on the family's educational experience is considerable.

Most parents claim that they try to be fair to their children, and not to do for one what they do not do for another. At first sight it may seem *unfair* to allow the first child to select the school of his choice and then expect younger siblings to follow on without debate. In fact, it seemed that in most cases brothers and sisters wanted to go to the school about which they already knew something from their elder sibling. This seemed to apply even if the older child did not like or was not doing well at the school. Perhaps their preference was expressed on the basis of 'better the devil you know ...'

However, it was not always the case that parents who put the child and his characteristics at the centre of the secondary school choice decision necessarily allowed him freedom of choice. Some parents tried to make a thorough going assessment of their child, in terms of his ability, health and temperament. Having formed a judgment of his needs, they cast about for a school which seemed likely to meet them. Whilst the child was usually consulted, his wishes were not the deciding factor. For example, they might conclude that he would make most progress in an all boys' school, the type of school whose discipline parents often anticipated would be stricter. Or he might be defined by his parents as 'an average child - so we looked for an average school'. In another case a daughter was felt to need 'a more intensive, pushing, work atmosphere', although her brother did not. Her parents concluded that one of the remaining grammar schools would best suit their daughter's needs. Only in the second of these three cases was the parents' assessment and named choice of school matched by the place eventually allocated to the child by the education department. Other parents, rather than concentrating their assessment on their own child, tried to make some assessment of the range of schools available. Several commented that private education had been briefly considered but ruled out as beyond the family's means. One mother actually put her daughter's name down at a private school, but had to withdraw it when her husband objected. More frequently, the otherwise unknown schools were assessed in terms of the subjects taught there. Parents rarely mentioned the booklet giving profiles of all the secondary schools in the borough issued by one of the local authorities, and had perhaps forgotten that they received it. Nevertheless, this booklet may have been the source of their information about subjects taught at the schools. Alternatively, they may have consulted the parents of children already attending these schools. A few of the parents took the opportunity to go to open days at several local schools, and one or two made individual appointments to meet headteachers and see their schools. One such parent commented: "The heads were chatty but surprised that before making our choice of secondary school we wanted to have a look round, and were interested to see what they did and what they had to offer the boy at that particular time. We got the impression it wasn't the normal thing to do. But we felt, with out first child going into secondary school, all we had to go on was hearsay."

Having formed some judgement of what the school had to offer its pupils, parents might further compare a few schools in terms of their lay-out (a split site often being criticised as facilitating truancy), their relation to the airport flight paths, and their nearness to the home. If the choice made following these considered calculations was not matched by the secondary school allocated, parents seemed proportionately more disappointed than if their abortive choice had been based on less complicated criteria. One parent said: "We wanted to make a knowledgeable choice - but the education department wasn't interested." Another commented that the idea of choice proved to be "a bit of a farce. List making was just a sop to parents."

These reactions point up to the fact that at the time of change of school, families who already have several years of involvement with the maintained system of education find themselves temporarily in no-man's-land. The children are *between* schools, in the majority of cases with no particular teacher involved in or concerned about what happens next. For the first time it is the education department, rather than the recognisable and known institution of the school which represents the educational side of the home/schooling equation. To most parents the department seems an impersonal, often an impermeable, protagonist. Its importance in family reckoning is usually short-lived, but the influence of parent/education department encounters is long term. Given that the department seems suddenly to emerge as an unknown but catalyst quantity in the child's educational career, it is not surprising that many of the brief encounters recalled by parents were stormy ones.

But parents who had been successful in obtaining their choice of school took a different view. One mother who had with the help of the primary school headteacher separately assessed each of her three daughters, requesting and obtaining different schools for them, felt at first that she had been 'lucky'. On second thoughts she concluded that she had in fact been realistic, naming schools which were suited to her girls' actual abilities and temperaments rather than to some idealised conception of these. Parents who did not get their choice of school, she concluded, must be fantasising about their children. (This was one of the many comments made by the parents we interviewed about 'other parents' whose perceived deficiencies evidently gave reinforcement to the speaker's own self-image.)

A few 'successful' parents attributed their achievement in getting their first choice of school to having expressed their wishes in terms that the education department would find acceptable, rather than explaining the real basis for their choice. One father of three already had two of his children at different comprehensive schools, schools X and Y. He was bitterly disappointed with school X. He said, "I was determined that the younger boy should go to school Y. So I put on the form 'has an elder sister at school Y'. I didn't mention his elder brother at school X!"

Before secondary school

We have discussed those parents who perceived the child's abilities, temperament or attitude as the crucial factor in secondary school choice and those who put first the facilities and attributes of individual schools. A small number of parents however based their choice not on the characteristics of particular schools, but on the type of secondary schools, but on type of secondary school organisation. These parents spontaneously declared themselves 'for' or 'against' comprehensives.

Almost all the secondary schools in both the boroughs where we researched were by then reorganised on comprehensive lines. The four schools on which we focussed were all-through comprehensives, ranging in size from 900 to 2,000 pupils. A few of the parents we interviewed actually lived outside the boroughs, in local authorities where comprehensives were still rare. These parents had made determined and successful attempts to get their child a place in a comprehensive school 'over the border', sometimes for the negative reason that they did not want their child to attend a secondary modern school; sometimes because they strongly supported the comprehensive ideal.

The core impression of a comprehensive school which both 'for' and 'against' parents seemed to share was that the comprehensive school accepted children of a wide range of ability who were taught in mixed ability classes, and that the atmosphere of the school was less pressurised than that of the grammar school. Apart from this basic commonalty of assessment, 'for' and 'against' parents tended to elaborate their description of the comprehensive school gave recognition to and encouraged all aspects of the child's abilities, valuing the practical along with the academic. Opposing parents felt comprehensive schools damped down all ability by working to a lowest common denominator and by eliminating competition. One of the latter group of parents considered such schools worked to the detriment of the working class, by eliminating erstwhile opportunities to improve one's position in life through the development and exercise of personal ability. Other parents thought that the whole atmosphere of the comprehensive school worked to encourage aspirations and development. 'The comprehensive has done away with the teachers telling them they won't be any good at things. They used to be afraid even to put up their hands - but now they are not afraid to speak out."

A few parents were so determined that their child should attend a comprehensive school that they firmly opposed their child's wish for, or even his allocation of a place at, a grammar school. "He cried when we wouldn't let him go to the grammar, but he saw our reasons," said one mother. Those reasons included not only a strongly felt politically affiliated support of the comprehensive ideal, but also the fact that the grammar school in question, being one of a very few remaining in the borough, was relatively distant from home.

For those parents who regretted the dwindling of the grammar schools, one comprehensive school was however not necessarily like another. The reorganisation of the local schools was relatively recent, and in some cases parents would name as their first choice the comprehensive which had previously been a grammar school. Such a school was felt still to have the aura of the grammar school, distinguising it from other comprehensive schools with differing antededents.

"I know the schools are all comprehensive now, but prior to that school O was a grammar school, school P was a secondary modern. I still believe that at school O you've got the grammar school concept coming out in the way they work, and at school P the secondary modern concept. You don't get the same volume of work out of school P." The parent quoted here was one of the few who had himself attended a grammar school. For most of the parents the move towards comprehensive schools represented not a sacrifice of past glories but rather an opening up of new opportunities.

The range of subjects now offered at the new comprehensive, compared with those taught at the secondary modern which the parents had often attended on the same site, was dazzling in its array. Parents often commented that the children could do 'anything' - the opportunities are all there'. The child's willingness to embark was often thought to be the only necessary factor, and there was very little recognition that internal organisational factors within the school might link some subjects or preclude others. These perceptions were to come much later in the child's school life.

In touching on the question of what the comprehensive school had to offer, we are approaching the question of parental expectations about secondary education to which we shall shortly turn. But before leaving the subject of secondary school choice, there are further points to make about the home and family factors which were almost always mentioned as having an important part to play in the process of choice, even if other factors appeared to be predominate.

The factor of the school's nearness to the home was a criterion mentioned by over three-quarters of the parents interviewed as an important influence on their choice. Those parents who gave no other reason than nearness for their choice of secondary school or who said that their children 'automatically' went to the nearest school seemed at first to be closest to the attitude of 'apathy' so frequently imputed to parents by educationists. However, the comments which more explicit parents made on their reasons for valuing nearness belie the apathetic stereotype.

The most frequently mentioned reason for choosing a nearby school was the saving of time and effort for the child.

Before secondary school

But parents were in some cases concerned about traffic and often wary of the need to rely on public transport. One comment summed up both these concerns: "If you choose a school nearby you haven't got to worry with bicycles or buses." Less typical reasons for choosing a school close to the home, each mentioned by one parent, were that to do so saved the local authority unnecessary expense (a parent governor) and that it was important for adolescents to get back quickly to the moral environment of the home (a Jehovah's Witness). More frequently, parents considered it important to be available to offer material rather than spiritual nourishment, commenting that because the secondary school selected was near at hand, the child could come home for lunch. One mother saw this as an 'essential break in the school day'.

Even if the nearest one at hand, the secondary school was unlikely to be as local to the home as the primary school had been. But there were a few parents whose choice of school went deliberately against the usual trend of including nearness as one of the factors of choice. We have already referred to Mrs. Morgan's determination that her younger boys should attend secondary schools out of the immediate area. "It is because of all this Effing and Blinding, if you will excuse my saying so," she explained. Another family, living in an outlying area of one borough, wanted their daughter to go to a school 'out of the village', which would provide a range of friends and new experiences.

The decision to try for a more distant school was usually made by the parents rather than the future pupils. But one far-seeing eleven-year-old now in the upper sixth, was described by her parents as having made, entirely alone, the decision to opt for a comprehensive school at a considerable distance from her home as she thought she would work better away from the children she had known at primary school. Her subsequent school career and academic achievement had been outstandingly successful. Her parents made no claim for their own influence in this, other than that they had not stood in her way.

Nevertheless, for most of the families nearness was a desirable if not the most essential characteristic of the secondary school of their choice. Despite the few bitter remarks about the 'sham' of parental choice, evoked by local authority allocation on what was perceived as neighbourhood principle, such a principle was not in fact at odds with most parents' wishes for their child at the age of eleven. For it was in the short-term that most of the reasons for valuing nearness were couched. Comments about the additional effort entailed for the child in going to a more distant school tended not to look ahead to the child's potential and imminent growth and development, but to assess the efforts in terms of the eleven-year-old. One mother summed it up: "To travel to secondary school means a man's day on an eleven-year-old's shoulders."

PARENTS EXPECTATIONS ABOUT SECONDARY EDUCATION

Much of what parents told us about their choice of secondary school made implicit reference to their expectations of what secondary education might or could offer their child. Whenever possible, during the interviews, we further explored this question of expectations, either in abstract terms or in terms of expected outcomes, according to the tenor of the discussion and the parents' preferred way of expressing themselves. In reflecting on what they had to say, it must be borne in mind that definition of all the parents interviewed already had at least one child at secondary school. Their expectations, although looking to the future, were already coloured and perhaps tempered by their experience.

The wide range of responses which parents made to enquiry about their expectations of secondary education tends to suggest that secondary education during the latter part of the nineteen-seventies was seen by parents as still in the melting pot. There was little indication that the child was seen passing through one stage in a homogenous continuous education system. However, the individual nature of parents' expectations may have derived not so much a perception of the educational system as unstructured and wide open to a range of outcomes, as to their perception of their own child, passing through the adolescent years, as bewilderingly unknown quantity.

Certainly many of the parents seemed to feel that whatever the secondary school might be offering, the outcome depended first and foremost on the child. Parents with several children stressed each child's individuality. They both expected them and found them to be different from one another,

We made some attempt to explore possible typification on the basis of sex, by asking parents whether their expectations about secondary education were the same for boys as for girls. Many wives referred to their own education or perceived lack of it, at this stage in the discussion, and the influence which their education had had on their employment experience or prospects. Not surprisingly, given that the enquiry came from a female university researcher, the great majority of fathers as well as mothers claimed that they felt girls' education to be equally as important as boys, although once again 'other' parents were referred to as being known to hold less enlightened views. Nevertheless, some interesting points did emerge about expectations regarding secondary education for girls and for boys. Once again these expectations were coloured by experience. For example, many parents obviously had had expectations that certain subjects such as cookery, woodwork or metalwork were sex-specific. They had been surprised and without exception pleased to find that these subjects were open to both boys and girls, and for many parents it was now an expectation that both their sons and their daughters should gain some experience in an untraditionally wide range of practical crafts.

A more abstract notion, expressed in terms of expectations about girls' education, was the double utility of their education not only for their own lives and work but future-orientated towards the children on whose upbringing it seemed to be assumed the mothers of the next generation would remain the major influence. So far as the girls' own development was concerned, there was some indication that although secondary education should be provided on a similar basis for both boys and girls, girls could be expected in fact to get more out of school. Sometimes this seemed to be because girls were perceived as settling down more readily to education. Boys were seen as needing and often *having* longer to develop skills, or as being more able to fend for themselves and take up opportunities in the working world that followed school. Whereas a boy might take up an apprenticeship or learn a trade *after* leaving school, several parents hoped their daughters would acquire actual employment skills such as typing as part and parcel of their secondary education.

It was in the discussion of expectations that we sometimes got the first indication of some of the ups and downs in family-rearing which contributed to parents' perceptions. Parental disenchantment with their teenage children may be seen by the outsider as an expected and temporary phase in family life, but to the parents' comments about their expectations regarding secondary education were more than a little tinged with fatalism, cynicism, disappointment or weariness.

"It's the children that much have the expectations, not the parents, if anything's going to happen." "I don't expect the school to turn a sow's ear into a silk purse." One parent had the general but somewhat jaundiced hope that his children would emerge from secondary school with a broad idea of what they were wanting to do in life. He became more specific: "For my eldest son - I hope he will try and find his own way. But you've chosen a difficult example - *I* don't know what he wants to get out of his education - and I don't think he does."

But some parents denied they had expectations about the outcome of their children's secondary education for very different reasons. One mother felt out of depth and overwhelmed by her child's success at school, and did not presume to have any particular expectations, since her child's achievement was already so in advance of the average. Another mother, the last of whose ten children was just passing through secondary school, seemed from her comments about each member of her long family to have taken throughout the role of kind and interested observer, who had no expectations in advance of her children's abilities and interests, but took developments as they came. Far from disinterested or apathetic, she nevertheless did not spend her strength in anticipating or pushing her children's development. Her theme was, "It's up to themselves." For just one parent, the whole idea of having expectations about secondary education was too passive an attitude. She felt the parent must *share* the role of educator, if much was to happen during the secondary school years.

However, the majority of parents did find it reasonable to have expectations about their children's secondary education. Some recognisable categories emerged from the interviews. Each was voiced, in not dissimilar terms, by several parents, and many parents had expectations which ranged over a number of categories.

One category was that of *social and welfare expectations*. This included the expectation of secondary education as an enjoyable and happy experience, of the secondary school as a place of safety while the child matures, and the more explicit expectation of 'social education'. An aspect of this was the opportunity for the child to be with his own age group, and to learn to get on with a range of people including adults. When the secondary school was seen as a potential source of social education, it was sometimes expected that this would spill over into out-of-school hours, offering children useful occupation in the evenings in the form of clubs, classes or opportunities for community activity.

Another expectation was that of *secondary education as a transitional educational phase*. Parents with expectations in this category appeared to have a clearer perception of an educational *system* than the majority of parents interviewed. Their expectations were expressed as 'an academic education', or in terms of 'subjects', leading to further and higher education, which in term was likely to lead to specialised work.

A further category of expectation was that of *secondary education as a phased introduction to the outside world*. References we group under this category were to opportunities to acquire a variety of job experience and knowledge, to be educated in the rights and duties of citizenship, to learn to cope with life and to become 'level-headed'. Very closely linked to this category but in some ways distinct from it were expectations about vocational guidance, advice and help for secondary school pupils. These *counselling* expectations overlapped both with the 'introduction to the outside world' expectations and also with the 'social and welfare' category.

Before secondary school

A more specific expectation was of *secondary education as job preparation*. This implied the acquiring of actual employment skills (especially by girls, as we have noted above). Within this category come parents' hopes for an opportunity to obtain a suitable passing-out certificate, summarised as exam results or 'a piece of paper'. When seen in terms of job preparation, the point of acquiring such qualifications was more often 'to show you have done it' than because the qualification would actually be useful at work.

An expectation which several parents expressed was that of *secondary education as an individually tailored experience* for their child. This was subtly different from those more numerous parents who thought that what one could expect from secondary education depended on the child, since they could only get out of it what they put into it. Here the expectation was rather that the child's potential would be studied by the school, and his educational experience would be tailored to the fulfilment of that potential. Parents who took this view felt their child's time at secondary school should not be one in which he experienced frustration because of inadequate or discontinuous teaching. 'Proper" provision should be made, so that any ability inherent in the child could be developed.

A category of expectation fairly frequently referred to was that the secondary school would provide *basic education*. By this broad term parents seemed to imply literacy and numeracy. One parent explained it as 'what you need for form filling'.

Some parents expressed their expectations in terms which indicate the category: *secondary education as time-serving*. Formal education was seen by these parents as an inevitable process, from which one was let out at the end. They did not always imply that the experience would be an unhappy one, but it seemed largely irrelevant to the real business of life.

There seemed to be little expection of *secondary education as a change agent* in the child's life, although there was some recognition that changes might well occur during those secondary school years, if not particularly because of them. However, a few references were made to intentional change, such as the expectation that secondary education would 'broaden the child's horizons' - beyond those of the parent, seemed to be implied. Or it might bring about change by providing encouragement to the child to fulfil his latent potential, or by enabling him to get an interesting job (unlike his parent, it seemed once again to be implied). One or two parents expressed the hope that the school would bring about change by 'pushing' the children.

Expectations of *secondary education as an opportunity for the accumulation of knowledge* were occasionally voiced. This was more likely to be qualified as knowledge which might come in useful. The idea of learning for learning's sake was extremely rare, though not entirely missing.

Very little expectation was expressed by parents of secondary education as providing *moral* education or *character training*. Even less was *religious education* expected. All of these were thought to be more the task of the home. But the term 'social education' was, as we have indicated, quite frequently used, and this was sometimes described as entailing 'respect for others as individuals'. One parent mentioned the values of honesty and hard work in this context. It may be that the tendency for parents to expect social education rather than moral or religious education at secondary school is more a change of terminology than of substance.

Those parents who were briefest on the subject of their expectations about the secondary school were those who said they expected it to provide *a good education*, and by this they appeared to mean a range of subjects. Here again, there may be overlap either with the category of secondary education as the accumulation of knowledge, or with secondary education as a transitional educational phase.

In our discussion so far, we have attempted to show that parents see their children's secondary school years as part of the fabric of the family's whole educational experience. In particular, the primary school years contribute to parents' growing knowledge of their child's abilities and temperament. From that knowledge, and coloured by their own experiences of formal education, they choose the secondary school, which they approach with a wide range of expectations. We now turn to an account of their interaction with the school, during the child's secondary school years.

Chapter Four

PARENTS AND SECONDARY SCHOOL TEACHERS IN CONTACT

Eighty teachers at four comprehensive schools took part in the research study which led on to the home interviews with parents. Before turning to parental perspectives on secondary schooling, we therefore briefly set out the views which teachers at the four schools expressed about home/school relations. We examine the extent to which these views reflect the changing rationales for promoting home/school liaison put forward in recent years and summarised in Chapter Two.

The four schools studied all professed eagerness to promote teacher/parent contact, and laid a great deal of stress on the occasions when parents could be involved with the school. Each school offered a series of parents' evenings, usually with a different evening for each year group across the school, once a year. The arrangements and formats of these varied, and were being changed even during the study. In one of the schools the form tutor was available to discuss the pupil's general progress and attitude with parents, who could also if they wished make appointments for more specific discussions with subject teachers. In other schools the evenings were principally to discuss the progress of the child in different subjects. Parents' evenings in three of the schools were linked with the periodic school report about the child. Sometimes they also took on the characteristic of an open evening, with demonstrations and exhibitions.

In addition to these regular events there were age related occasions at each of the schools - such as a careers evening in the fourth or fifth year, an option choice evening at the end of the third year and evenings for parents of children who had only just joined the school and those who were about to do so. Concerts and school plays were major events with an appeal not simply to parents but to a wider audience still.

Each school had either a parent/teacher association or simply a parents' association, and this usually made itself responsible for convening several social and fund raising events, as well as for business and educational meetings. Each school had its own governing body, and during the study parent governors were being introduced and elected. One of the schools was experimenting on a limited scale with enlisting parents' help during the school day.

All of the schools had arrangements whereby parents could fix up a meeting with individual teachers to raise matters of concern with the teacher, and each school retained the right to invite individual parents to the school to discuss educational behavioural problems. Communication via letter and telephone appeared quite rare, except in arranging such meetings. None of the schools had a policy of home visiting, although in a very few cases individual teachers had taken the initiative to visit a home, usually about educational rather than disciplinary concerns.

These then formed the range of contact points between teachers and parents. In the majority of cases the meeting place was the school and the initiative for contact lay with the school. Few teachers lived locally, and the possibilities for informal encounters in the shops or in the street were extremely limited.

In discussing the aims and functions of a relationship between home and school,[1] teachers ranged over the whole spectrum covered by the home/school literature. They pointed out that contact with parents might enable teachers to learn more about their pupils' home background, encourage parents to take an interest in their child's school work, and show them how they could help their child at home. By being in contact with parents, teachers could find out whether the aspirations of the home were congruent with those of the school, and they could appeal to the parent body to give its support to the school as a whole. Through their contact with parents, teachers could try to generate local respect for the school, and perhaps get parents to identify with the school as a neighbourhood institution. Teachers also suggested that such contacts provided an opportunity for parents to express their appreciation to teachers, and for teachers to render account of the work they undertook.

The schools varied in the emphasis which they laid on particular purposes of home/school relations. In one school, the chief aim was to generate parental interest in the school,

---

[1] This account is chiefly based on four research documents prepared in collaboration with the teachers concerned. These documents (nos. 1/172, 2/200, 3/203 and 4/175) were cleared for wider circulation following the research, and are obtainable from the Educational Studies Unit, Dept. of Government, Brunel University.

and in another to improve teaching and disciplinary practice through increased understanding of pupils' home background. Overall, however, the objectives voiced were child-centred. Parental interest in the school would encourage the child; improved teacher understanding of home background would aid child development, by enhancing teaching and disciplinary handling.

The aims emphasised by all these teachers were in fact those promoted by the home/school literature of the nineteen-sixties, and gave some evidence of the cultural lag in absorption of new educational ideas in unexceptional schools.

Although the benefit of the child was ostensibly at the centre of home/school links, the thrust of home/school policy in practice was towards enlisting parental backing for the school as an educational institution - enabling its smooth running and enhancing teachers' sense of their work being valued and supported. It was also evident that the incentive to know more about pupils' home background was chiefly related to difficult pupils. Teachers at one school pointed out that some of the difficulties which pupils caused at school should be defined as parents' problems rather than teachers' problems. This could be more authoritatively conveyed to parents if teachers had at first hand knowledge of the home background and its presumed deficiencies. The need to understand the home background of pupils who presented no problems at school was evidently, and understandably, less pressing.

At another school, teachers acknowledged that there were certain benefits in meeting the parents of amiable cooperative children. The appreciation which such parents expressed was encouraging to teachers. These were the kind of parents whom teachers perceived as responding most regularly to school invitations. Nevertheless, parents of below average ability pupils, these teachers implied, would have more to gain by coming to meet teachers.

Whatever their hopes for and belief in the value of home/school relations, teachers at all four schools expressed disappointment about the level of parental response to school invitations, and were broadly critical of the attitudes and lifestyle of their pupils' parents.

Throughout the sequence of research discussions in the schools, it was evident that teachers were ambivalent about what type of parent and what type of parental participation was the most desirable, from the point of view of the school. They wanted to modify supposedly indifferent parents, and encourage them to become supportive educationally appreciative parents - the 'families educogenes' defined by Floud (Halsey (ed), 1961). Nevertheless, they did not want parental interest to be stimulated to such an extent that parents would seek to intervene in the 'professional concerns' of the school. In the teachers' eyes, the role of parents whose children attended these neighbourhood comprehensive schools was to support the school rather than criticise. And in relating to parents, teachers defined their own role as to educate parents about school aims and practice, rather than to understand the parents' values and priorities. This was nowhere more clearly conveyed than in the remarks which teachers made about the shift work in which many parents were involved. The implication was always that parents were at fault in undertaking to work these hours, which considerably restricted opportunities for family contact. There seemed to be little recognition by teachers that shift working was a ubiquitous requirements in many spheres of employment locally available.

Very few of the teachers who contributed to the research seemed to feel at ease with the neighbourhoods in which the schools stood. The teachers at one school unequivocally pointed out that 'the majority of parents belong to lower socio-economic classes than the majority of school staff.' It was difficult for teachers who did not live locally to establish any rapport with what they defined as 'the larger mass of unconcerned parents'.

Teachers were disheartened by what they perceived as local apathy towards education, but they were in no doubt that the schools should continue to take the initiative in trying to improve the relationship between home and school. They showed considerable resilience and optimism in the new ideas they were prepared to formulate and discuss for strengthening links between home and school. Few of these proposals, however, seemed to address the primary interest of the parents (which teachers noted and acknowledged) in their own children. Although the teachers' own home/school objectives were ostensibly child-centred, teachers seemed always to be trying to wean the parents away from the propensity to particularise, towards an ability to recognise the overarching aims of the school and education.

PARENTS' CONTACTS WITH THE SECONDARY SCHOOL

Despite the catalogue of occasions which teachers described on which parents were invited to the schools, it was not uncommon for parents to say, in interview, 'I don't often go to the school - in fact there aren't many occasions when I'm expected to go.'

This lack of awareness of the full range of school events at which parents were welcomed may indicate a failure of communication between school and parents. But it can also be interpreted as a realistic assessment of the number of opportunities for parents to talk to teachers. From the teacher's point of view, a school's programme may entail a continual round of evening meetings or events involving parents, but for individual parents these occasions can be widely spaced. And parents may not count visiting the school for a play or concert as a point of genuine contact with teachers. Most parents considered these events as entertainments in their own right rather than as fund raising exercises or attempts to involve the parents with the school and its activities. Parents' evenings, however, were described in similar terms by both teachers and parents.

Parents' evenings. In the interviews with parents, parents' evenings were the single most frequently mentioned school occasions. It was clear that these evenings carried the burden of interaction between teachers and parents, and that the content of such meetings and the perceptions of parents about the role of these events were crucial in the relationship between family and school. Morever, as the principal channel of communication, parents' evenings fulfilled a diversity of functions.

Usually a report on the pupil had been prepared by the teachers in advance of the parents' evening, and a discussion of the report was the focus of the encounter in three of the schools. The evenings were clearly recognised as being about the progress of individual children, and structured round an information flow from teacher to parent. Parents' evenings were the epitome of what parents seemed to anticipate would be the context of a relationship between teacher and parent - a mutual concern for the child. These events explicitly devoted to a discussion of the child and his progress were, not surprisingly, the most popular and perhaps the most successful parent oriented events organised by the schools. Nevertheless, comments on the shortcomings of parents' evenings were illuminating.

It was apparent that some parents, realising that the event was a once-a-year occasion, thought there should be considerably longer time spent with each parent and far more of a heart-to-heart discussion about the child than was possible at most of the schools. Many parents who expressed this point of view recognised it as an unrealistic expectation when they saw how many people the teachers had to meet. But they remained convinced that teachers had a great deal of knowledge about their child which it would be valuable to tap and interesting to discuss.

It was clear that parents expected teachers to have a good deal to tell them about their child which they did not already know. And many parents, within the constraints of time available, were having their expectations fulfilled. Several commented, with some pleasure, on the revelation of a different aspect of the child's character such as helpfulness, which came out in school though not at home. Aptitudes too, might be evident at school which were not demonstrated at home. The discovery by parents who had no confidence in their own mathematical ability that their child was showing an aptitude for maths made the contact with teachers at parents' evening a positive and enjoyable experience. However, most parents' expectations moved beyond learning straightforward new facts about their children to the level of interpretation which they hoped the teacher would be able to offer. A substantial number of parents evidently regarded the parents' evening as a kind of clinic at which their child's character would be analysed and discussed in terms of a future appropriate to his talents. Parents were expecting teachers to be able to identify the particular strengths and weaknesses of their children and, more than that, to comment on the ways in which these could be best exploited both during the child's school career and subsequently in employment. Rather than to discuss a school report, which was essentially about hindsight, many parents were keen to direct the conversation they had with teachers towards the future and call upon the teacher's judgments about appropriate future directions. It was perhaps here that parents' expectations differed most from those of teachers, who did not claim to be providing personal guidance of this kind and who were not anxious to intervene in what they saw to be personal choices. The teachers' aim was chiefly to benefit the child by giving his parents a better idea of how he was getting on at school.

Parents attempting to form a total view of their child's life in school and what it might mean for the future were also expecting to have the opportunity to meet a number of his subject teachers. In this connection parents expressed satisfaction about the organisation of those parents' evenings which allowed appointments to be made, so that they could select which teachers they needed to see and when they would see them. A chaotic and poorly run parents' evening sometimes persuaded parents that this was not the most appropriate contact point with the school and some preferred to use alternative events, such as private interviews, to find out what was going on. In one school, the arrangement whereby parents talked only with their child's form teacher was seen as a limitation, but it was compensated for by offering a better opportunity for a thorough discussion about the child.

Three different interpretations were offered by parents about whether it was appropriate to use parents' evenings for the discussion of individual problems, including disciplinary problems, with the school. Parents who regarded the parents' evening as being about a discussion of the child's academic progress considered it would be necessary to arrange a separate, individual interview with the headteacher or other appropriate member of staff if there were any particular problems on which they wished to consult teachers. But there were other parents who thought the only reason for attending a parents' evening was to sort out problems, academic or behavioural. If there were no such problems, there was no reason to attend the parents' evening. In between came the largest group of parents who, recognising the meeting to be about a discussion of the child's progress in school, understood this to mean any aspect of the child's behaviour in the school and who, on many occasions, saved up problems until parents' evening to bring them to the attention of the teacher. This practice, which was widespread, may have reflected the parents' view that this was the only significant contact point between parents and teachers, although it may also have reflected a diffidence about making a special trip to the school or appearing to fuss over what might turn out to be a fairly trivial concern. In some cases parents themselves expressed surprise and disappointment that the teachers themselves had not used the contact at parents' attention. In one case there had been persistent truanting which the father only found out about by accident. Given his regular attendance at parents' evenings, he was alarmed to find teachers had not felt this was an appropriate opportunity to tackle such a problem with him.

Teachers were themselves contributing towards an expectation that at parents' evening they only wished to discuss problems. Many parents reported teachers saying to them, 'You're not the parents we want to see, the parents we need to see are the ones that never come,' implying that they wanted to see the parents of children with problems, so as to discuss those problems at the parents' evening.

We have seen that some of the teachers thought parents' evenings as the occasions when they demonstrated their accountability towards the consumers of their services. Some of the teachers were nervous about the parents' reaction to events which had occurred during the school year, and certainly considered they had to answer for the different performances of the children. Parents, however, did not seem to see themselves as exercising consumers' rights, and testing the standard of service at parents' evenings. If anything, the parents were more nervous about the event than the teachers realised. They felt they were being scrutinised by the teacher, and themselves held accountable for their child's performance.

There were, however, isolated examples of parents seeing the parents' evening as an occasion when teachers could be held accountable for the education of their child. One parent spoke of 'interviewing' the teacher. Several others had taken the opportunity of challenging the teacher about the wisdom of educational methods being used and expected some notice to be taken of their point of view. But accountability not only means being open to challenge, it has the more positive connotation of being found to have done the job well. Some parents evidently welcomed the opportunity to show how much they had appreciated the school's efforts, remarking that teaching was a thankless task and they thought the teachers deserved more appreciation.

The opportunity which parents' evenings provided for the teacher to learn something about the child's home background was a point made by many teachers, but rarely by parents. As a general rule parents did not anticipate that teachers would be wanting to find out a great deal about them at a parents' evening and might have been surprised to learn how much teachers depended upon this event for their picture of what was going on in the home. However, if parent and teacher got on to the subject of problems with a child's school behaviour or progress, it was apparent that the discussion frequently turned to the child's home background and parents were quick to volunteer information that they thought might be affecting poor school performance.

Although we have observed that the parents' evening may be multi-functional, the centrality of the school report in the encounter appeared to constrain some parents from widening the discussion. The parents of one well-behaved pupil complained that the teacher simply said 'I wish all the other pupils were like your daughter,' and went on to talk about the weather. But their daughter was intending to proceed to higher education and these parents were already out of their depth. They would have liked to talk to the teacher more generally about school subjects, and the changes that had taken place since their schooldays. Yet it did not seem to them that they could introduce this type of question into the discussion, and they remained in ignorance about new development. Awareness of the number of other parents waiting to see the teacher was another factor which inhibited parents from channelling the conversation into areas which might require full and perhaps lengthy discussion.

As the report on the pupil figured so prominently in the event, the value of parents' evenings to parents was closely bound up with the report, and how useful this was found to be. Here parents' experiences varied considerably. About a third of parents found the report less helpful than they wished. For some, the very inadequacies of the report encouraged their attendance at parents' evening, so they could find out what the teacher really thought. Yet for others, the lack of knowledge of the pupil which the report conveyed made them feel there would be nothing more the teachers could say - they obviously did not know the child well.

But a majority of parents found the reports interesting and helpful. Approval was often expressed of the 'cheque book' system which was being adopted in the schools, whereby a separate sheet was filled out by each subject teacher, and a conclusion drawn by the form teacher. This form of report highlighted the variation in effort which teachers put into the report and their different levels of knowledge of the child. Parents found, however, that the different quality of comment tended to reflect the child's own interests and enthusiasms, since an indifferent comment often went hand in hand with the child's own indifference. Nothing could reflect more accurately the interactive process of teaching.

Some parents were positively glowing in their praise of teachers' judgments. 'They've got him down to a T!' one father proudly announced. And a considerable number of parents could lay their hands on the latest report, or successive reports, to show researchers what the teachers had said.

The overall impression gained from parents about parents' evenings was of a bustling event where discussion might have to remain at a fairly superficial level. Parents worked out their own strategies to make the most of the time available. Many felt they should identify the 'important' subjects and make sure they saw those teachers; others tried to pick the ones where their children were having problems. Husband and wife teams divided the teachers between them, or else prepared themselves as if for a marathon.

<u>The pattern of attendance at parents' evening.</u> Around 80% of parents interviewed claimed they had attended one or more parents' evenings (a proportion similar to that noted by Lynch and Pimlott, 1976). About half the parents had settled into a routine of regular attendance at parents' evenings, although not necessarily for all the children in the family.

A small number of parents made attendance at the evenings an absolute priority, rearranging shifts or even taking time off work to be able to go together. Many more said they would make sure that either father or mother would attend, and there had to be a very good reason if they decided not to go. Both these sets of parents regarded attendance at the child's parents' evening as a parental obligation which they sometimes found difficult to explain in purely instrumental terms.

For some parents whose children were getting on well at school, the occasion had something of the character of an annual ritual, at which it was not doubt pleasant to hear about the performance of their child, but which placed some strain on the teachers to think of something novel to say. Whilst it was almost heresay to consider not attending, a number of such parents observed that they wondered why they did still go, since they heard the same story every time. But among the 50% attending on a regular basis there were also many parents whose children were not necessarily amongst the school's success stories and where there was a great deal more to say than 'doing nicely'.

Many parents in the category of regular attenders not only had a feeling of parental obligation, but were also responding to their child's wish for them to be present.

Speculating on what would happen if they decided to discontinue regular attendance, parents said this would disappoint their children, an observation which might have surprised those teachers who regarded the pupils as indifferent, if not actually hostile to their parents' attendance at school. But here they perhaps underestimated the curiosity amongst pupils about what the two or three most significant adults in their lives would talk about. Parents testified to their children's fascination with what the teachers had said about them and it appeared most of the parents obliged by passing on, with due discretion, to their child what the teacher had said. For the ten or twelve parents who said their children did not like them to go, three times as many alluded to 'not letting the child down' by missing the evening, or attending in correspondence with the child's wishes.

Among the comments made about parental obligation was the frequently expressed view that if a parent shows interest, the child has more reason to be interested in his or her own school work. Approximately a fifth of parents saw their attendance as providing motivation for their child and emphasized this rather than their own personal satisfactions. Attendance was an outward sign to the child that the parent valued education, and it was meant to be read this way.

Schools may have been more successful than they realised in conveying the view that it is the parents' duty to come to a parents' evening held at the school. Even those parents who never or rarely attended felt they should offer some explanation about why they did not come. An explanation commonly offered was that both parents were out at work all day and were really too tired in the evening to consider going out to the school. Others pointed to the fact that the report seemed satisfactory and so there was no necessity to go to the school and discuss it. In contrast, two or three parents felt the report was so bad there was not point in going. Some said they had attended one or two meetings at the start, to make sure the child had settled in all right, but after that there had been no need to attend. Some intermittent attenders asserted that there were certain crucial meetings one had to attend, for example when option choices were discussed, but that apart from these the routine parents' evenings were a matter of 'take it or leave it'. One of the schools had evidently succeeded in conveying their 'open school' policy since a number of parents said parents' evening was not the only occasion at which to discuss the child's progress, and they would not hesitate to make a special arrangement if they thought this was necessary.

Other reasons stated for lack of attendance included having to look after young children in the family, being a long way from the child's school, or finding a clash between the programme of one school's activities and that of another.

Whilst some of these took on the characteristic of an 'excuse', in most cases they appeared genuine. The dislike of going alone (the complaint of a few mothers and one father) was also deeply felt, as was the rather bitter experience of one couple who no longer went, that the teachers were only interested in the brighter children.

Without abusing the status of our data by suggesting regularities backed by statistical analyses, certain associations were observable in our study and these might be worth examining in a wider survey. For example, separated parents living on their own attended parents' evenings less frequently than the average, but there were notable exceptions when such parents were straining hard to make sure their child did not 'suffer'. Practicalities figure here, given that there was no one else at home to look after young children, or that the single parent had both a full-time job and a home-making role. Practicalities again seemed to be as much as a feature in the slightly lower than average attendance rate of parents with families of four or more children. And parents with children over a wide age range were more likely to attend only intermittently, except when the children at secondary school represented the younger children of the family.

Although we did not systematically gather information of mothers' and fathers' employment, a working mother in the family appeared to tie in with a lesser involvement with general school activities, but it was chiefly how this linked with the father's working life that seemed to affect attendance at parents' evenings. One fairly active mother who worked part-time in the evenings was only absent from the parents' evenings when the father was also away on business. A lack of fit with shifts was also frequently mentioned as a reason for missing a parents' evening. What is entailed for the family which makes a regular appearance at parents' evenings at a secondary school? There appear to be two main factors.

Firstly, there is the characteristic of making an arrangement ahead and, with appointments systems developing, seeking and fulfilling appointments with particular teachers. Secondly, it is necessary simply to be able to be physically present at the event. Whilst the schools we were dealing with were, it seemed, increasingly taking on the characteristics of neighbourhood schools, some of the parents lived at some distance from the school. The areas where the schools were located were characterised by a high proportion of shift work among the working population and so the conventional evening meeting was not always convenient. Arrangements had sometimes to be made for looking after younger children, and there was quite a spread of ages in the families we contacted. Each of these practical problems could present major difficulties in a family where both mother and father worked. The cards are stacked in favour of the small mobile family, accustomed to organising its life in a routine and formalised way.

Any sense of pleasure in the parents' evening as an event was related to establishing 'rapport' with the teachers. One parent seemed to echo teachers' views when he said bluntly - 'They're different from us. I would not choose to spend my time with a teacher socially - nor would a teacher be that interested in me.' But no parent openly suggested that class differences between parents and teachers prevented them from putting in an appearance at parents' evenings. It was suggested to Lynch (Lynch 1976) by parent respondents that differences of speech inhibited working class contact with teachers, but this view was not made explicit in our study. As if to discount this suggestion, several parents stressed how much the teachers made them feel at home. Nevertheless, parents' evenings do not seem designed to meet the needs and convenience of manual, shift workers, and the content of the encounter may prove more manageable, manipulable and intrinsically satisfying to parents whose education matches that of the teachers. What is remarkable is, not that a small but significant proportion of the parents interviewed did not attend parents' evenings, but that so many of them did.

Other school events. Whilst the parents' evening was the most successful event among those intended to draw parents to the school *en masse*, the schools were also looking to displays, fund raising events, social events and talks to involve parents in the life of the school. Teachers took parents' attendance at these as just as much a sign of their support for and interest in their child's education, and schools were attempting to improve the frequency and the quality of contact with parents by promoting such events.

It was apparent, however, that most parents had a different outlook on these other occasions. Few saw them in terms of support for the school or support for education. At events where children were on show, such as plays, concerts and sports days, parents' attendance was mostly linked to the appearance of their own children. Whilst a few parents said it would not matter if their child was taking part or not since they liked to encourage the other pupils, a majority of parents explaining their attendance at a concert or display referred to their child's involvement. Attendance was a product of the relationship between parent and child, rather than parent and school.

Contact between parents and teachers was in any case fairly limited, on such occasions. There might be a brief introduction by the headteacher, and teachers might feature in the production or at least be in attendance, but it was scarcely an opportunity for parents to get to know teachers better or vice versa. Nonetheless, these events had potential for cementing cordial relations. Parents were obviously gratified at being recognised and greeted by teachers, or being complimented on their child's performance. And the school sometimes became a venue for the whole family on such occasions. If a pupil was in a school show it often brought out mother, father, aunts and uncles, grandmother and next door neighbour. Pupils could be seen showing off the school (and, at a distance, their teachers) to a wide range of interested relations. As a means of increasing knowledge of and identification with the school as an environment, these events were perhaps more effective at getting to other influences around the child than parents' evening.

At one school, plays and concerts were achieving a reputation for good entertainment value that took the significance of these events further, giving them a potential for school/community relationships that perhaps the other schools would have envied. In a deprived area, so far as entertainment was concerned, the major school plays, which were usually musicals, were thought by many to be 'as good as the West End'. Parents referred to having to buy the tickets quickly before they were all taken, and the audience included those with only the most oblique connections with the school. Although this was perhaps exceptional, there appeared to be a good turnout at most 'entertainment' based events at all the schools, and whilst the stated purpose was frequently in connection with the child, the undoubted enjoyment they created played a part in ensuring parental attendance.

Social events, which often doubled as fund raising events, provoked a different response again. Here, the dominant theme among parents was that attendance at these was a matter of individual taste or preference. These events were seen more than any other school-based happening as orientated towards parents as individual adults, rather than being linked to the child. If parents found these congenial, then it was appropriate to go, but if they did not, the *child* was not the loser.

The great majority of parents interviewed were not regular attenders of social and fund raising events although they may have contributed indirectly by sponsoring walkers, sending jumble or providing produce for stalls. The attitude that it was a question of personal preference was more often voiced by the non-attenders - 'Can you see me standing there with a little finger cocked in the air supping wine?' Even if it was not made explicit, it was implicit that 'I am not that kind of person ...' However, some regular attenders also considered this sort of activity might or might not have appeal, depending on the parent's personality.

Absorption in school based social activities, it became clear, was often an alternative to substitute for other types of voluntary activity. Two mothers had been active with cub scout groups. For various reasons one mother withdrew from her cub scout responsibility and instead found herself active with the school. Then her involvement in the townswomen's guild gradually grew. At the time of interview, there was a switch in interest from the parents' association to the townswomen's guild, which she thought a more suitable outlet for her energies, given that her children were almost grown up. The other mother tried to fit school activities around her scouting responsibilities, but found they often clashed. In another family, a mother had entered wholeheartedly into school based concerns. She gave the impression she had been looking forward to her children's secondary schooling to give her more scope, and she had specifically dropped other voluntary obligations to enable her to enjoy the schooling centred ones.

In all these cases, whilst there were undoubtedly deeper motives, the participant was certainly deriving some satisfaction and pleasure in her own right, and, on the evidence, would have been involved in equivalent, though non-school-based, associations if her child had not been at secondary school. It is perhaps no coincidence that the most striking examples are of women, several of whom were not at work, or who had part-time jobs. These mothers found school related activities stimulating, and convenient to their domestic timetables. Several other mothers who had been active at primary school, which was often a period when they had not been out to work, and who would have liked to maintain their interest at secondary school level, found their working hours did not now permit such close involvement.

Parents' associations. Many of these activities were linked with parents' associations. The official ethic of these associations was not personal enjoyment, but service and loyalty to the school and its pupils. Many parents did not share this view, however. Describing her first attendance at a parents' association meeting, a mother referred to 'finding out whether it was my kind of thing' and several others who did not continue attendance had come to the conclusion it was not. The widespread expectation was that such meetings would be found to be sociable and that one would feel comfortable with other parents, not simply because they were parents, but because they would be compatible friends and acquaintances or would become so. If the association proved to be 'cliquey' (a common criticism) or if one did not have friends or find it easy to make friends, one would be unlikely to find the parents' association congenial. Although the comprehensive schools had some characteristics of neighbourhood schools, the locality they served was considerably more far reaching than the catchment area of a primary school. A number of parents who had been active in primary school associations found at the comprehensives that the enjoyment of doing things at the school was not the same when they did not already know the parents of their children's fellow pupils. They dropped out of the parents' association for this reason.

Several activists resisted the interpretation that belonging to the parents' association was a matter of personal pleasure, and they deplored the shortsightedness of fellow parents for thinking that the association merely offered a variety of social activities for which individuals had a taste or not. They stressed that it was equally a parent's responsibility to show interest and loyalty to the school, in less direct ways than parents' evenings, and noted that although the focus of activities was not the benefit of the parents' own child, other pupils in the school would benefit. This in itself should constitute sufficient motivation for parents, in the views of the activists.

The thorny question of how parental activism might benefit particular children was faced up to and treated in different ways by involved parents. Some denied that there was any chance of influencing teachers in their own children's favour through such involvement (and the relative lack of involvement of teachers at some of these events added unwitting substance to these declarations); others naturally accepted their own child would benefit, but attributed this to the child's own increased interest in school if the parents became involved. One or two parents frankly admitted their child might get an increased share of attention, but thought this was not to be wondered at, since teachers would be bound to try harder if they knew the parent was also making an effort. The accusation that active parents were trying to curry favour with teachers was in fact rarely voiced by non-involved parents. However, not all association events were explicitly social. One parent/teacher association, with educational objectives to the fore, was becoming quite active in assisting the school to present sessions for parents about subject teaching in the school. These occasions were not so far proving to have wide appeal. Yet it was apparent that such events occasionally tapped more than the interest of the die-hard activists and, for example in technological and science matters, drew on the interest of fathers who had not had close involvement with the school. Even so the limited attendance was a little unexpected in the light of parents' puzzlement with new methods and content of teaching. Perhaps the answer was that whilst a few parents claimed to be interested in knowing more, a greater number by far were resigned to the developments in the curriculum and felt it was not possible to keep up. In fact, it was a matter of pride to many parents that their children had overtaken them in their learning. 'It's all beyond me now' was a phrase repeated by many parents, sometimes with resignation, sometimes with awe. The intricacies of methods and the complexity of school equipment became things to marvel at, and not attempt to understand, and many parents implied it would be presumptuous to expect the teachers to be able to explain it to them. Nevertheless there was a strand of curiosity among parents which such explanatory sessions might eventually draw out.

Ad hoc contact. A focus of our wider research study was the school's responsibility for the welfare and personal conduct of pupils. From the teacher's point of view, this seemed to be the aspect of the teacher's work which would most benefit from contact between home and school. Nevertheless only a minority of parents had ever had ad hoc contact with teachers about problems of pupil behaviour. Whatever the reputations of modern comprehensive schools, the schoolday is not one of perpetual trouble, and the majority of behavioural peccadillos are contained and dealt with in a routine way inside the school.

In principal, however, almost every parent interviewed thought it appropriate for the parent to be involved by the school in anything more than minor breaches of discipline, and expressed a willingness to cooperate with the school in sorting problems out. When asked whether it was right to involve parents in disciplinary procedures taken by the school, a typical response was that it was only commonsense to do so, since the procedures would then be likely to be more effective. A strong implication was there were resources (and by this parents did not mean physical punishment) open to parents which teachers did not have. Furthermore, many parents simply wanted to know if their child was misbehaving, and two or three families were disenchanted with the school for not telling them straight away about suspected truancy. A repeated theme of discussion was the opportunity to 'nip in the bud' any tendencies to anti-social behaviour or truancy. 'On report' systems and regular checking with which the parents assisted were approvingly mentioned as successful examples of disciplinary partnerships between parents and teachers.

Nevertheless the hypothetical nature of some of the parents' answers about their willingness to cooperate must not be overlooked. For most of the parents, this willingness had not been put to the test. And in a few cases where parents had been contacted, the seeming triviality of the offending behaviour had not endeared the school to the parents. A father had to take time of work to go to the school to deal with something he regarded as a classroom offence which any teacher worth his salt could deal with. Although he still took the view that he would wish to be told of offences in future, he wanted to be sure that the teachers had exhausted their own resources before 'dragging him in'. And several parents, although happy to be involved, interpreted school-based problems as partly the teacher's fault. Ensuing action was not so much a question of teachers and parents collaborating, as of parents advising the child how to cope.

Mostly, parents who had been to the school to discuss disciplinary cases had done so at the school's invitation. Some parents, however, obviously received letters about disciplinary offences without going to discuss these further. Whether the letter had suggested a visit to the school was not made clear. None thought it unreasonable or unnecessary for the school to have approached them. A family whose children were proving particularly difficult and disruptive claimed they had installed their telephone to make it possible for the school to ring them. Whether or not this was true, with some families where there were persistent offenders among the children, contact had become quite informal.

It seemed less common for the schools to have taken the initiative in contacting parents over 'educational' matters. The parents' evening was the main vehicle for this kind of contact. However, there were a few examples of a teacher getting in touch with parents about educational concerns, as when a girl had decided to drop Latin and the school contacted the parents to suggest she kept it on.

Very few accounts were given of teachers having visited the home, but where this had occurred it had been in connection with subject teaching rather than welfare. One teacher, who admittedly taught a subject in which there was more personal attention and smaller classes, dropped in on two different families to discuss the child's progress and what the parents could do. This had been greatly appreciated.

When parents took the initiative in contacting teachers it was far more likely to be educational concerns than disciplinary problems which provided the stimulus. Among the problems that had taken parents up to the school to sort matters out had been discontinuous maths teaching (mentioned several times), many different problems to do with P.E. teaching (improper kit, forced showers etc.), putting the child in for CSE instead of O level (again a very frequent point of discussion), the lack of notice taken of homework, and so on. An abiding theme of these complaints was to do with the school's arrangements for teaching, rather than about content. This may be because the substance of lessons was thought to be a matter for the professional judgment of teachers, or because much of the content was a mystery to parents, whereas organisational arrangements were much more open to parental scrutiny.

Difficulties in fitting in different optional subjects were a frequent cause for concern, and often of disillusionment with the school. For a number of parents, the range of subjects taught had influenced their decision concerning the secondary school for their child, but then they found a certain combination of subjects could not be fitted in. Option choices should be recognised as the first occasion, subsequent to the choice of secondary school, at which hard and binding decisions are made about the child's future and about the child's relative success in the school. Whilst exceptional problems in these areas appeared to have affected only a handful of families in our study, relatively minor difficulties over option combinations seemed to researchers to have had a general effect in bringing the 'honeymoon' period with the school to an end. The lack of responsiveness of the school to their dissatisfaction confirmed some parents in the opinion that the school did not care about what parents thought, and brought home to some other parents the realities of the schools' limited resources to a wide range of pupils.

Parents did also occasionally take the initiative in approaching the school about disciplinary concerns, such as alleged unfair treatment, the discovery of truancy, children getting into bad company and behaviour deterioration. There were perhaps fewer complaints about the first type of problem than teachers seem to think. It was clear from conversations with many parents that their children were not afraid to tell them about the trouble they had got into in the course of the day, and that not infrequently, children dwelled on the injustices of it all. But only in extreme cases did parents take action. In a few cases, parents had certainly leapt to the defence of their children, and there were tales of heated exchanges with teachers. But equally there were descriptions of amicable outcomes, with schools agreeing to separate children, to reconcile teacher and pupil and so on.

It was apparent parents had thought carefully about visits to the school over disciplinary cases when the nature of their complaint affected other pupils. For example, at one school there appeared to be a spate of bullying, and several parents were having to grapple with what they should do about it. A common outlook was that it might only make things worse for a child if complaints were made and several parents were being exhorted by their children not to interfere. Parents, it seemed, were prepared to take action on behalf of their child, but in most cases were weighing the advantages and disadvantages of what might then ensue.

THE MECHANICS OF PARENTAL APPROACH TO THE SCHOOL

In a later chapter we discuss the trauma which a visit to the school may represent for a parent. Here, we shall consider how the parent makes contact, whom they think it is appropriate to ask for and whether parents feel encouraged to approach the school.

All the schools had developed pastoral systems which were intended to provide appropriate routes of enquiry concerning all aspects of pupils' school lives. In no school did the headteacher insist that he was the initial reference point, and some made a point of informing parents which member of middle management on the pastoral side should be approached about problems. The parents' response to these often complex systems was usually to circumvent them, however unconsciously. There were two distinct strategies. One was to ask to see the particular teacher involved with the problem, or else the child's form teacher. The other strategy was to start at the top with the headteacher every time, as a matter of courtesy. Both strategies assumed there would be filtration, either upwards or downwards, but the parents' view of the initial point of contact often confounded even quite simple pastoral systems.

Of course, the parents could be confounded too, since their initial contact was highly unlikely to be a teacher at all, but the school secretary. In one school in particular she took on herself the responsibility of advising parents whom to talk to, when the parent could do so and what to do next. To some she gave the impression of a sympathetic go-between, while others felt she prevented them from speaking to the particular person they wanted. To a lesser extent, school secretaries in two other schools performed the gatekeeper role, at least with telephone communications. In the fourth, the very size of the school had persuaded many parents that the best thing to do was to ask the secretary to advise them whom to contact. Parents at this school seemed to be coming to terms with the size and complexity of the school by *not* insisting that they would have to speak to the headmaster.

But several parents, especially in heated moments, visited the school without warning and then the layout of the school had an impact on whom they might see. In two schools, the secretary's office was still the most prominent point of enquiry, but the others had a more complicated geography. Parents might be aiming to reach the headteacher, but from their accounts of such impromptu visits proved more usually to have spoken to the member of staff based nearest to the school entrance, or someone whom they encountered in the corridor.

Parents' views about the receptivity and approachability of the school are often formed during the type of individual encounter we have been discussing, as much as by the formal encounters such as at parents' evenings. In ad hoc encounters the schools were occasionally and inadvertently giving an impression altogether different from the one they would have wished. Most ad hoc contacts between individual parents and teachers occurred not over important behavioural and disciplinary matters, but over what were for the schools day to day occurrences - things like lost property, minor accidents and incorrect uniform. Because they represented routine matters for the teacher, though not necessarily for the parents, teachers adopted what some parents interpreted as a careless attitude. The loss of an expensive jacket was a worrying event for a family with a tight budget, and in many parents' views, called for a rather more concerned reaction amongst teachers than the comment that 'With all the pupils there are in the school, it is impossible to keep track of individual pupils' property.' Experiences of this sort could convey the impression of a school insensitive to individual problems, and some parents automatically inferred from this a less than caring attitude to the child in other contexts. Also the response of a particular teacher could colour a parent's attitude to the whole school. This might be favourable or unfavourable, although the frequency with which a negative picture was conveyed was higher than schools might expect.

In one parent's account, a teacher had declared in a resigned tone that he 'could not control the kids', and the parent had been quick to interpret from this an unprofessional attitude on the part of all the teachers. In another case, a teacher had responded to a request for some homework for an ill child in a very offhand manner, which gave the impression the school was not prepared to put itself out for individual pupils. One teacher, mixing up two pupils at a parents' evening, persuaded a parent that teachers just do not get to know individual pupils.

Perceptions varied enormously about the permeability of the school, and the value of approaching teachers over problems. One father proudly announced that the school had instantly followed his instructions to part his son from a bad influence, and thus was confident that there was some point in making one's view known to the school. A mother who had persistently suggested how the school might get on better with her daughter, with a series of what sounded to be highly practical suggestions, sadly noted nothing had changed. For some parents there was the feeling of coming up against a soft cushion, on which one could make no permanent impression, among others the suggestion of a remote institution in which parents' views were not wanted, yet among another group still, the feeling that teachers took considerable notice of what the parents said. But those battering their heads against a cushion did not necessarily give up, and those detecting a responsiveness did not always take their problems to the school.

The relationship between home and school is not solely the product of experience through formal and informal contacts. An important contributory factor is how the parents interpret their own stage in life, and their position in relation to their children. In the next chapter we turn aside from the school to examine the familiar role of the parent during the secondary school years.

Chapter Five

PARENTS AND TEENAGERS

Social scientists have tended to view the parent and child roles as prescribed, carrying certain enduring attributes and being subject to well-established role expectations. The parent/child relationship is certainly one set of role relationships in which the participants have little choice. The relationship is one that can rarely be escaped from or repudiated. But the apparent permanence of the obligations created by the roles masks the dynamics of parent and child coming to terms with one another over a period of time. The relationship develops and changes even though the child remains dependent upon the parent, and the demands of co-existence with a child of five years old are radically different from the demands of co-existence with a fourteen-year-old.

Changes in legislation have lengthened the period of time during which a child is expected to be dependent upon the parents, financially and emotionally, but society's norms of parent/child interaction have barely changed to take account of the increasing complexity and variability of such lengthened relationships. It may not be easy to fulfil society's expectations about the proper role of a parent when the child is young, but it is perhaps even more difficult when the parental role is being played out in relation to a lanky, possibly unattractive, thoughtless adolescent, who is encountered as much as another independent human being as a child. The parents we met were well aware that with children at this age their parental role was no longer the same.

Changes in family relationships during the secondary school years. Many of the mothers and fathers we interviewed, including those dubbed by teachers and social workers as uninterested parents, were thoughtfully negotiating their relationships with their children. These negotiations were not always successful, but few parents were simply taking either the parental role or the child role for granted. There was no accepted blueprint for dealing with the possibly increasingly recalcitrant or increasingly remote and mysterious young people they found in the midst of their family. Parents were having to come to terms with young people asserting their independence, but still highly dependent upon the home and family.

The majority of parents accepted their relationships with their children would have to be different from the relationships they themselves might have had with their parents. While they might have preferred what they saw as the certainties of that older kind of relationship to the uncertainties of creating newer forms, the realities of contemporary society and the expectations of their children about the relationship were forcing them to rethink. It was also apparent that the child's transition to secondary school was an opportunity for re-appraising the parental role, and for parents to reassess what their children were like. It may have been that the occasion of talking to researchers was the first time many parents had articulated their approach to parenthood, but it was certainly not the first time they had confronted the issue of what it meant to be the parent of a maturing 'adolescent'.

One of the difficulties surrounding parent/school relationships is that many teachers' expectations about parents' responsibility for their children are based on a model more appropriate for the parent and primary school child. The assumption that parents stand in the same relationship to their secondary school child as they did during the primary school years is one that needs to be questioned.

<u>Parents' responsibility for and influence on their children.</u>
Parents' feelings about responsibility for what the child has become, and for what the child is like now, profoundly influence their view about whether it is appropriate to become involved in school affairs, from disciplinary misdemeanours to more formal and regular contact through parents' evening. At one extreme, some parents considered themselves entirely responsible for their children's development and behaviour. Others, in contrast, judged their influence on their children to have been minimal.

To those parents who felt they took complete responsibility, since theirs was the major influence on the child up to and into adolescence, it appeared entirely legitimate that teachers should bring the child's failings to their attention and expect them to take action. Behaviour in and out of school was interpreted by these parents as being their full responsibility, since the child was what they as parents had made of him. Several parents emphasised that if their child was truanting or misbehaving, there was no point in blaming the school. In nine times out of ten, the problem would be with the home. In most cases where we found parents accepting this degree of responsibility and, in some cases, blame, it seemed to be associated with a sense of accountability which was reflected in other aspects of their life. Such parents were disinclined to talk of luck and chance, or to give the impression of being blown by fate. They were also disinclined to look outside the family for support or help.

If their children were successful and well-adjusted it was of course agreeable for parents to accept full credit and take pride in their children's achievements. However, there were as many parents with successful children who appeared pleasantly surprised by their children's achievements, which they in no way attributed to their own efforts. These parents tended towards the opposite end of the spectrum, where the individuality and separability of the child from its parents' influence were more likely to be stressed.

The extreme end of the spectrum of parental views about their influence on their children is reached with those few parents who did not feel they had been a significant influence on their children, although this did not automatically mean that they abdicated responsibility for them. These parents often seemed genuinely puzzled by their children. Confronted by the undeniable variation between the children in one family, it was not surprising that many parents felt their own influence to have been small. Either they felt the child had been open to many other influences from an early age or they felt the child was not susceptible to influence. Whichever of these interpretations they offered, parents stressed the individuality of their children and their relative independence.

Bewilderment about how children could have turned out so different had led some parents to revised their previously held views about their own influence. Parents' responsibility, they now concluded, was an aspect of basic parental duty rather than specific responsibility for what the child was and had become. Such parents might therefore continue to maintain a relationship with a school, not in the expectation of being able to influence the child or through any feelings of accountability for what the child did, but because of their perception of general parental duty.

Intermediate between the more extreme positions is the one occupied by many parents who felt responsible for certain characteristics of their children, but who were also conscious of other wide-ranging influences on the child's development and no longer detected their own influence as outweighing others.

The school as an influence on the child. Discussion of other influences at work on the child showed that many parents saw the school itself as one of the chief additional and, in some cases, alternative influences. The parents' view as to whether the school represented a supportive or alternatively a harmful influence was an important factor in home/school relationships.

Several parents pointed approvingly to the formative influence of a particular teacher or particular school environment. Sometimes they expressed rueful gratitude for this influence. 'He took far more notice of her than me'. 'By all accounts he was much better behaved at school than here at home.' 'He will do anything for the teacher' - were common types of remark. But the recognition of a beneficial influence exerted by the school did not necessarily lead to an inclination to have more to do with it. Some parents thought it best to leave the school to get on with its work and recognised that the child might well prefer not to have this separate environment invaded by the parents. But equally, some parents wished to become associated with the school and its influence, and learn from the teachers' dealings with the child. Many parents we encountered were highly appreciative of the advice teachers could give them and, as the child became increasingly remote, turned to the school as another source of information about their child and how to deal with him or her.

The school as a countervailing and harmful influence was not a dominant theme in the majority of interviews with parents. But when parents did see the school as an unwelcome influence, the chief criticism was often related to the matter of discipline. The school as an environment seemed to these parents to reflect lower standards than the home. They pointed to the informality that reigned at school and deplored the lack of respect that this seemed to engender. Some parents were appalled by the way in which their children addressed their elders and the way in which they referred to teachers. The school, these parents claimed, was not only failing to enforce standards which they were trying to maintain in the home, but was failing in its duty to equip pupils for life outside the school.

It is often publicly stated by teachers and others that parents expect the school to enforce disciplinary standards more rigorous than those maintained in the home, and the comments above might be interpreted in this light. A few parents certainly conveyed the impression that the school should be the source of discipline rather than the home. Some of them referred to the lack of discipline in schools as if the division of responsibility between the home and the school was that the home delivered the child to the school, rather like raw material to a factory, on which the school subsequently operated by filling the child with knowledge, good manners and an acceptable standard of behaviour. But these parents were definitely in a minority, and many parents went out of their way to stress that they did not expect the school to do what the home was not prepared to.

Another group of parents, again in a minority, conceived the difference in influence between school and the home in moral or religious terms. Most parents expected a certain generally accepted morality to pervade the school, which they equated with the kind of morality they tried to convey at home. Whilst several parents were devout families the lack of moral education perceived in the school was cause for real disappointment. As one Muslim explained, he did not expect denominational instruction and, indeed, he would have been satisfied for his sons to receive an essentially Christian outlook since he was confident he himself would be able to inculcate correct Muslim beliefs. Furthermore, he did not believe the moral instruction of the two religions to be substantially different. But the lack of any instruction he felt severely hampered his own efforts in educating his sons and in teaching them proper respect.

<u>Parental perspectives changing over time.</u> The importance of the attitudes described above as being on a spectrum from a feeling of complete responsibility to little or no responsibility for the child's characteristics, is how they are sustained or how they gradually change as the child matures. By the secondary school stage, parents increasingly realise that they have to come to terms with the developing independence of their children, and this may mean that their attitude to the school is modified to an outlook that accepts the independence of the child. There was inevitably a certain amount of ex post facto explanation about children's autonomy, after they had engaged in misdemeanours in school. But several parents reported consciously correcting their impression of their child's independence in the light of certain revealing episodes, which had demonstrated the child's continued reliance on parental guidance.

Some parents felt strongly that their young adolescent children remained influenced by and dependent upon them, but that the nature of this influence was changing, or that they had to be more discreet about using it. In contrast, a few were conscious that their children were insufficiently independent and made efforts to encourage them to stand on their own two feet and take decisions for themselves. Others detected an autonomy which was age-related. 'They think they're independent from the age of 8. They're not, but you've not got to let them know that. But by fourteen or fifteen, they really are, there's nothing you can do about it.' Some associated the age of independence closely with the age of transferring from primary to secondary school, although again, it must not be assumed that such parents abdicated responsibility for their children at that age.

<u>Changes in family relationships influencing parents' views.</u>
We referred earlier to the possibly inappropriate model that teachers may have of the parent/child relationship, which then affects what they expect of parents. It appears that many teachers are assuming a parent/child relationship more appropriate to the primary school school years of children than secondary school years. The assumption is that the parents relate to the children and take responsibility for the actions of children in the school as if the pupils were entirely dependent upon their parents and, in extreme cases, not accountable for their own actions. Although in Chapter Four we reported that parents mostly wanted to be involved in serious disciplinary cases, several parents disapproved of the way teachers brought them in. 'They expect you to go running up there whenever something goes wrong. Why can't they sort it out themselves? It's not up to me to sort him out. The teacher has got to deal with the child directly and not expect me to deal with him for them.' Teachers themselves were in a position of authority over the child. When they turned to parents for help in controlling him they seemed to be looking for reinforcement in their own approach to the problem. But although parents reported wanting to be involved they sometimes took a different line from that of the teacher. Many referred to their wish to exercise guidance, but not to impose authority. Whilst teachers may have seen this as a weakness, parents saw it as an attempt to come to terms with the child's adolescence, and to give the child a sense of self-discipline. Some parents considered teachers created problems by dealing with the pupil as a child, rather than as a maturing adult. Recognising the child's developing maturity, they felt, would do two things. It would be likely to lead to a more successful teacher/pupil relationship between teacher and pupil, and it would make it less necessary to call in parents if the relationship broke down.

Some parents felt constrained in their relationship with a school by the very tendency of teachers to associate them closely with the children. They wanted to dissociate themselves from their children in the teacher's eyes in an effort to get the teacher to see that the child was moving towards responsible independence.

Whatever the intricacies of meaning of teacher/pupil interaction, its dominant motif is the dependent role of the pupil/child. Parents wanting to bolster their child's confidence and self-determination could well find it desirable to retreat from a relationship with the school and encourage

the child to take direct responsibility for his/her actions
vis-a-vis the teacher. Moreover, too close a partnership
between teacher and parent could look remarkably like
'ganging-up' on the child. The difference between this and
pooling experience to achieve a desired outcome, that is
modification of a child's behaviour, was sometimes difficult
to establish. One or two teachers were conscious of this, and
were most reluctant to invite parents to join with the teacher
simply to put more pressure on an already pressured child.
But one parent ruefully admitted that neither the school nor
the home had much effect, and all the relationship between a
teacher and parent did was to reassure both parties that they
were not alone in their frustration when dealing with the
child. This relationship was sustained largely for the
therapeutic value to the parents and teacher, rather than for
the child.

Several teachers described the dynamics of parental
involvement with the child's school as a display of interest
by parents at the beginning of the child's secondary school
career, followed by a slackening of interest thereafter, with
a pick-up at the time of decision-making concerning options
and examinations. It is appropriate to examine how true this
picture is, in particular whether the beginning of secondary
school life for the child marks a special stage in the
relationship between parent and school.

<u>Differences in the part played by the parent when the child
moves from primary to secondary school.</u> Our earlier discussion
of the primary school years first identified the phased
withdrawal of parents in an effort to encourage their children
to be independent and self-confident. As the change to
secondary school looms, some parents find themselves
confronted with a dilemma. They do not necessarily want to
become more intrusive or reverse a direction that they
consider desirable, but they may fear that in the secondary
school, the child is facing a strange and possibly
overwhelming world which he or she is ill-equipped to manage
alone. But equally, they may appreciate that only if the
child learns to cope with it will he settle down. The
solution for many parents is to take a great interest at the
beginning of secondary schooling, but with the intention of
withdrawing as soon as possible. Hence, there may be an
intensive round of visits to the school, preparing the child
for the change to secondary schooling, with follow-up visits
shortly after the child has begun, and then what the teachers
see as a slackening of interest, but which may be a tactical
retreat.

Some parents managed the changeover with marked
discretion. 'I knew she wouldn't have wanted me to go with
her on her first day, so I followed discreetly behind her

without her knowing, just to make sure she got there all right.' This was a parent who was worried about her child's lack of self-confidence, and who wanted to encourage her child at every opportunity to make her own decisions whilst still wanting to offer the stability of parental interest.

Teachers drew attention to a change in the type and style of contact which parents had with their children's primary and secondary schools. Mostly they thought this was characterised by a less active involvement with the secondary school, and we found several cases to back this up. For example, one family had made a conscious decision to change its pattern of involvement. The parents had been active in the primary school PTA and, in fact, had been instrumental in setting it up. However, they decided not to take an active part in the secondary school PTA. At the primary school they had not been happy with the degree of interaction between parents and teachers and had seen the PTA as a means of persuading the school to be more open to parents. But the secondary school to which their child was going already had an active PTA, and a welcoming attitude towards parents, so they no longer saw the need to be so active. This was an instance where the parents' perception of the characteristics of particular schools influenced their actions.

But other parents expressed their different approach as having more to do with the change in their children than in the characteristics of the school. Some parents saw a dramatic change in their children as they moved from primary to secondary school, and this was a change to which they felt they must respond. Several parents, who at primary school had gone in to help by listening to pupils reading and been regularly present at school-related activities, thought their children would be far less keen to have them involved in the secondary school. 'The relationship changes because the children change. A new relationship has then to be worked out.'

However, a reduction of interest was not the only direction of change. There were several instances where parental interest increased when the child moved on to secondary school. One mother went along to an early PTA meeting, was persuaded to stand for the committee and became involved in a way that she had never been at primary school. And membership and activity in a PTA might well seem a more appropriate way of showing interest in the child's secondary level to parents who felt it was wiser to withdraw from a direct and possibly cloying relationship with the child whilst still wanting to be supportive.

<u>Fathers and the secondary school.</u> Of greater significance is the potential upsurge of interest amongst fathers in the secondary schooling of their children. This phenomenon was

referred to by both mothers and fathers we interviewed. The change was often perceived as relating to the nature of education at secondary level, either because the father was more familiar with its content, or because it was considered to have a more serious and relevant purpose than primary education, thereby warranting more serious attention. Many fathers, and for that matter mothers, regarded the primary school years as being more of the mother's concern and the problems thrown up in the course of primary schooling to be domestic ones which the mother could sort out. Furthermore, seeing the child to and from school was more often a mother's task, and the kinds of events for parents were orientated, in style and in timing, principally towards mothers. One mother commented that her husband stopped going to primary school open nights as he 'couldn't put up with the queuing up while mothers yattered on to teachers for hours about their little Julia, rather than just checking up on progress.' But he was ready to start going again now their son was in secondary school.

Parents perceived the content of their discussions with secondary school teachers becoming increasingly technical and job-orientated. In these matter, families generally agreed that the father was more likely to have experience to offer which enabled a more purposeful discussion. Some wives were so nervous about talking about these 'unfamiliar' matters that they insisted their husbands went instead of themselves. In other cases wives recruited their husbands to go along with them. And many wives whose husbands could not come along found the idea of conversing with teachers so disquieting they no longer went at all.

It was not necessarily, or even usually, the case that wives had to persuade their husbands to take an interest. Many fathers appeared pleased that their children's education had reached the stage when they could show an interest and derive some satisfaction from contact with school. They felt they had a valid point of view, based on experience, to offer alongside the teacher, particularly over careers. Several fathers working in industrial settings considered they had a more accurate and up-to-date notion of the opportunities open to girls than either their wives or the teachers. Others were fascinated by the subjects being taught at secondary schools, for example, two fathers mentioned the developing subject of geology.

Another factor in the increased involvement of the father at this stage of schooling was that, although many of the parents left school at a fairly early age, in some instances the fathers had had a year or two longer in education than their wives.

The child's transition to secondary school and his or her new status as a secondary school child, can then, be a time of reorientation both within the family and in connection with the school itself.

Parents' experience of the value of parent/teacher contact. The parents' relationship with their child has been central to discussion so far and must remain so, as long as we accept the argument advanced by most educationalists and by the majority of parents themselves that the child is the central point of interest in a relationship between parent and teacher and that the child is the beneficiary of such a relationship. Do parents' experiences back this up? Do they go along with the implied passivity of the child which the notion of parents and teachers getting together to achieve certain desired outcomes for the child conveys?

'The children who do well are the children whose parents show an interest in what they are doing' is a generally accepted piece of wisdom. But it is rather too easy to assume a causal relationship - 'You've got to show an interest as otherwise they will lose interest', 'I feel sorry for the kids whose parents show no interest, they're bound not to do so well', 'You can see very clearly which are the kids whose parents show an interest'.

Some parents were conscious that the two things were not necessarily connected and one father actively disputed the accepted wisdom. He referred to the fact that 'teachers always talk about the kids who get into trouble as being those from a poor home background, whose parents they never see.' What led him to dispute this statement was the fact that his own son had got into severe trouble, and was seemingly in the middle of a career of disruptive behaviour. The father was genuinely puzzled by this, although by no means inclined to disclaim responsibility. He explained that he and his wife went regularly to the school on open days, parents' evenings and so on. They were supportive of the school, both at an individual level with their own children, and through offering help directly to the school whenever appropriate. When asked what difference parental interest and support made, he found he honestly could not say. So far as his daughter was concerned she had settled into school, had a successful school career, and been a model pupil. It could be deduced from this that parental interest had been benign. But thinking about his son, it could not be argued that the demonstration of parental interest had made one bit of difference. On the basis of this experience, he felt he could not support the view that it is the children whose parents show no interest who go astray, and he claimed that since he had made this discovery, he had come across colleagues at work and other parents who had arrived at similar conclusions.

In another family the mother had always been involved in a routine way with school and had developed an interest in the PTA. In about the second year of secondary schooling, her son had started to play truant and display extreme hostility to the school. She had then become closely involved with the relevant pastoral teachers, and had long discussions with them about what to do. These discussions were continuing, but the mother had few illusions about their impact. 'It doesn't make a bit of difference to him. But I find it helpful to at least discuss the problem with someone else, even if all we do is agree that we can do nothing about it.'

In both these cases psychiatric help had been recommended by the school. Yet the behaviour pattern of these pupils was not highly untypical and in most other cases would not have led to the offer of psychiatric help. What was untypical for the school was that the families concerned seemed to be the types of families from which highly conformist and successful children emerged. The definition of these children as 'abnormal' can be seen as an attempt to maintain the school's view that disruptive children come only from uninterested families. If a disruptive child comes from an interested family, teachers conclude there is something much more seriously wrong. The father in the first case characterised this suggestion of psychiatry as bringing in a hammer to crack a nut, perhaps conscious of the fact that his son's behaviour was not unlike that of many other pupils.

<u>The effect of the child's school career and progress on the home/school relationship.</u> In most of the child's school career, the child himself is the chief interpreter of school to the parents. The parents learn most of what they know about the school directly from the child. And, in connection with most parent/teacher contact, the child is the intermediary. It is usual practice for schools to dispatch routine information to parents through notes to be carried by the children. Some schools had adopted the newsletter format to communicate regularly with parents, but again, this was carried home by children. Many teachers speculated whether the majority of such communications reached home, but parents appeared to be satisfied that most did, even if they were accompanied by offhand remarks such as 'You won't be interested in this ...' or even if they only came to light from rummaging through pockets. Hence, the child's attitude towards contact is another critical factor in parent/teacher contact and parents were well aware of this. But, perhaps more crucially, the child's school career itself is an important determinant of the pattern of home/school contact. The child's conduct may cause concern or not, but either way it forms the focus of discussions between individual parents and teachers. Whilst many teachers commented they regularly saw the same parents year after year, the steady progress of a pupil led one or two parents to slacken interest and many more to consider not attending parents' evening.   A child's

eventful school career may either lead to a much more intensive relationship than that envisaged when a child started school, or may be the critical factor in discouraging parent/teacher contact. It may intensify the relationship either through the parents' own concern stimulating them to arrange meetings with relevant teachers. A number of parents in the former category were quite accustomed to responding to the school's invitation to 'come up' (an educationalist once remarked that all schools appeared to be built on hills) and have a word about a problem, but for them this was the only point of contact. One family, described by the school as a 'problem family, relatively uncooperative and not too interested in their child's school career', appeared to consider it quite normal and acceptable for the school to get on to them whenever it was concerned about the children. Neither parent had ever considered going to parents' evening or open days, but, willy nilly, were far more involved with the school than many other families.

For some parents, the initiative of the school in these instances reassured them and got over the problem of their taking the decision to contact the school. Several parents specifically disclaimed feeling resentful when the school asked them to come up to discuss a problem. 'I was pleased. It showed they cared.'

The progress of the relationship between parent and school in these discipline cases depends on the role the parents adopt towards the school. They may see themselves as mediator between teacher and child, intercessor on the child's behalf, champion of the child's cause, or supporter of the school versus the child. But if parents feel unable to play any of these roles, the child's erratic school progress may actually discourage the parents from any form of contact with the school.

One example of this concerned a sensitive and fairly diffident mother who had been quite closely involved with her children's primary schools. As the primary stage came to an end she began to look forward to a social life based round the child's secondary school, meeting other mothers and joining the PTA, but was rather too shy to make the first moves. Then her children began to come home with less than satisfactory reports, referring to a lack of concentration and flippancy. Whilst she desperately needed reassurance on this and spent much of the research interview discussing the problem, she was conscious of what many other parents referred to, the reflection that this poor report made on the parents and the suggestion, which teachers would deny making but which many parents found unavoidable, that they as parents were to blame. Other parents in this position took a rather more robust view - 'There is a sense in which you feel they are criticising you through criticising the child, but you've got to feel so bad about it.' But in this case the mother had become afraid of going to the school, feeling vulnerable to such criticism. There was a strong suggestion that, if the children had had more successful school careers, she would have found the potential interview with the teacher less harrowing and this would have been the first step in a closer involvement with the school.

This case highlights the fact, often seemingly overlooked by teachers, that the parents of school children are individuals in their own right, with needs and expectations like any other human being. The school encounters them simply as parents of X pupil and thereby begins the process of identification objected to by many parents and pupils. Even though the parent approaching the school does so also as a parent of X pupil and, indeed, because of this relationship, there is nevertheless an individuality and identity which may be seeking expression. Many parents were quick to spot this individuality in teachers (perhaps because their children talked so much about individual teachers and their separate characteristics). But teachers appeared slow to similarly recognise the individuality of parents.

It is not unreasonable to speculate that the satisfactions and therefore the tendencies to sustain a relationship depend upon mutual rewards. A totally altruistic relationship, implied by the expectation that the whole purpose of parent/teacher interaction is the well-being of the child, is not a full reflection of the realities of the relationship. There is liking and disliking in their relationship, there is fruitful discourse, which reassures the participants that the purpose of the relationship is being served, and fruitless discourse. There are fulfilled and unfulfilled expectations.

Chapter Six

WHAT THE SCHOOL ASKS OF PARENTS

One of the hidden and relatively unexplored aspects of the home/school relationship is what goes on in the home in support, in complementing or in opposition to the school. Teachers speculated on this and on certain occasions tried to advise parents what to do at home which would help the child at school. There were in any case certain things which all parents were expected and required to do in support of the school - ensure their children's attendance, cooperate in the matter of homework, and supply the school with necessary information about the family. This chapter discusses the attitudes of the parents interviewed to these "required" activities. Our research also gave insight into other kinds of parental activity which parents thought of as supportive to the child, which could in many instances be rather different from what teachers were expecting. These are described later in the chapter.

<u>Parents' Attitudes to their children's school attendance.</u>
Parents' later attitudes to school attendance cannot be adequately assessed without some reflection on the effect on family life of the earliest years of compulsory schooling. Parents had of course shared their parental responsibility before their children started school. Children had been left with relatives, friends or neighbours, even with paid baby-sitters or child minders, but rarely with professionals in an institution with premises like those of the primary school, where the child not only had to go, but could in most cases be relied upon to be kept, for a number of hours each day, while parents got on with other things. The school holidays, as a dimension to be reckoned with in family life, immediately began to mark off and punctuate the year into half-terms and terms. Parents' freedom to go to work and the family's freedom to go away on holiday, became structured by

What the school asks of parents

the school's yearly routine.

Of course, this is not to say that school attendance requirements become, for most families, central and immutable facts of life, governing all family arrangements. Many families exercise their right to take their children away on holiday during the school term, and keep their children away from school for shopping trips, outings and visits to relatives. But once a child in the family is of compulsory school age his schooling, like his parents' employment, plays its part in structuring family life. For some this new dimension constitutes a beneficial extension of family members' activity; for others an irritating interference with the idiosyncratic tenor of private life.

For the great majority of the parents interviewed it was taken as a matter of course that the school must be notified of the reason for any absence of the child from school. The school was accountable for the child's daily presence and must be 'covered'. One mother commented that it was 'only good manners' to send a note, but most of the parents seemed to contact the school when their child was away more in the spirit of keeping their side of a bargain. 'Of course the school must keep check on where they are', said one mother. And a father commented, 'Give an explanation if they are missing a class or away. They wouldn't accept the child's word.' The absence note, for most parents, was a required part of home/school cooperation, and they could understand the reason for it. 'There's quite a bit of truancy about, and it's the school's way of stopping it.' One mother was quite clear that the obligation was a two-sided one. 'If the child is sick I always write a letter to the school. And I tell the school that only with my authority may the child be sent home. When I send my child to school I am expecting her to stay there. It is not that school is a looking after place, but it should be a place of safety and learning. Children should only be allowed out if there is a letter from the parents requiring this.'

While many parents felt the school needed to 'have it in writing' that a child was away for good reason, others felt that sending a message by one of the other children or making a telephone call to the school secretary were suitable alternative ways of letting the school know. In one case of an asthmatic boy his mother had been told she need no longer send a note – the school knew why he was away. Parents seemed to experience some variation in the rigour with which their requirement to notify the school was, in the event, checked up on. Sometimes notes had been written when the child returned to school, but were found not to have be handed in. But in other cases 'even after one day's absence the teacher looks for a note'. Children might get 'told off', or get a detention if they did not bring a note. Or the school might send a form to the parent to fill in if they had not written a note when their child returned to school.

While the unquestioning acceptance of the need to explain children's absence from school was the attitude most widely noted in our interviews with parents, there were some parents who seemed particularly anxious to make sure that the school understood the child's absence was justified. In several cases parents both telephoned the school while the child was away and wrote a note when he or she went back to school.

One mother used to request a certificate from the GP for her child to take back to school with her note, even though the certificate had to be paid for. She wanted the school to know that her child had been absent 'for a good reason'. A father commented that if their daughter was ill or away from school his wife would write a note or telephone immediately. They never kept her away unnecessarily as they 'didn't want her to antagonise the school'. A few pupils, mostly in the lower forms, seemed to take a similar attitude. Parents remarked 'she likes things done properly'. 'She wouldn't go back without a note - they do seem to make a little thing of it at the school.'

A number of parents remarked on the extreme reluctance of their children to stay away from school, even if unwell. 'Even if they're a bit down, they always say, "I must go to school",' said one father. For one family it was 'a fight' to keep their son at home if he was ill. And one boy was set on going ' even on crutches'. In the case of these determined attenders there was no particular indication that they were apprehensive about the consequences of staying away, but simply that they were keen to get to school despite difficulties.

Not all regular attenders had quite this dedicated attitude, however. One girl who never missed school had tried to persuade her mother that it would be all right to have an occasional afternoon off for shopping, as many of her friends seemed to do. Her mother's response was to try to get her to accept that an unwavering attitude to school attendance was part and parcel of getting the most out of education.

These parents and pupils who were ultra conscientious about school attendance were only a small minority among those we contacted. As we have said, the most common attitude was of an obligation to keep the school informed about the reason for the child's absence. Most parents did not expect the school to query the validity of the reasons given, which covered a fairly wide range. While much the most frequent was the illness of the child, the illness of a parent, especially a mother, was sometimes cited, and in one case a boy was kept home to keep an eye on an ailing sister, while his mother went shopping. Sometimes work being carried out in the home required the presence of a family member. A father explained: 'We had some work done in the house recently. Someone had to be here. Either of us would lose money if we stopped away -

What the school asks of parents

so I had to keep the boy home - it was the lesser of the two evils.' One mother felt that if her son at primary school got two days off for some reason, it was only fair that her daughter at secondary school should have a holiday too (and she would be able to keep an eye on her brother while the mother was at work). But by the second day the daughter had decided she preferred to go to school.

Sometimes, however, parents themselves were dubious about the validity of allowing their child to stay home from school. Illness was an obvious justification, but parents could not always be sure that symptoms were genuine. One mother said that so far as she was concerned 'they've got to be dead to stop home'. This seemed to be more because of her own obligation to go to work (which she felt she could not do if the children were home ill) than because of their obligation to go to school. Another mother, although doubtful about the genuineness of her son's complaints, was more prepared to compromise. 'Sometimes he feels like a day off - but I say no. But if he says he has a bad head, I have to give him the benefit of the doubt.'

Several parents, if they came to the conclusion that their children were trying to get out of going to school, tried to find out the reason for this, and often made an attempt to arrive at some joint solution to the child's problem with the school. One mother of a child in first year got in touch with the school to explain that the child was frightened of having to read aloud in English, and asked for extra reading help for her. However, parents sometimes felt that their intervention might make matters worse. One girl, described by her mother as a 'timid little thing', made unsuccessful attempts to get out of going to school on days when she had RE, as she was upset by the teacher shouting, not at her, but at the other children. Her mother debated whether to go up to the school about this, but decided it might do more harm than good.

Particular lessons seemed to be the most identifiable cause of spasmodic attempts to avoid school, but parents did not always consider this an adequate reason. One mother was shocked by her daughter's 'fraudulent behaviour' in developing 'imaginary illnesses' on certain days when she had lessons she disliked. However another mother was prepared to dignify her son's indispositions with the label 'psychosomatic', when she learnt that he was being bullied at school.

Actual episodes of truancy by children for whom this behaviour was untypical were sometimes the cause of considerable concern to parents. One father felt that his son's preferred reason, dislike of a teacher who 'flicked him round the head' was just an excuse, but he continued to try to find out what was affecting his son, and whether anything was really bothering him at school.

For some families equally determined to keep their

children in regular attendance at school, however, the idea that children would try to get out of the school building, or avoid going to school at all, seemed much more natural tendency, which it was up to both parents and teachers to combat. One mother considered that especially during the period of the middle teens there should be close liaison between school and home. 'If there is going to truancy, it will be in that age era. But if the child knows you're interested and will *find out* if he's not at school - he won't truant.'

Some parents had been reluctant for their children to attend a split-site secondary school as it was too easy for the children to wander off when changing from one building to another. 'This is not good for children - if they can get out they often will,' said one father. The particular opportunities for getting out of another of the schools studied were well recognised by parents and also by the teachers. A mother with three boys at the school said, 'A great many of them do go in and get their mark, then come out through a hole in the fence. I've seen the headmaster and his deputy around there in their cars, picking them up!' She added, 'Mine wouldn't dare - they'd know how *I'd* feel about it!'

The right and duty of the school to contain their children and the principle of the compulsoriness of education was not seriously called into question by any of the parents interviewed. These children of the 1970s were the fourth and fifth generation subject to compulsory education in this country, and their parents seemed to accept the school years as an inevitable if not necessarily an enjoyable phase in their children's lives. '*I* had to go to school - they have to go to school,' said one father. Parents often compared their children's obligations to go to school with their own obligation to go to work, and the procedure of writing a note and explaining absence from school was felt to be the same as 'getting a day off' from work. Getting out of going to school, like getting out of going to work, was sometimes described as 'skiving', and absenteeism was frequently referred to as something that children should not 'get away with'. One pupil, present at the interview, considered it was much easier to 'get away with' at his present school than in Kenya where he had spent his earlier school years.

But although parents did not question the principle of compulsory education, they were not always in agreement with its duration. Most of the parents had left school at fifteen, and some at fourteen or earlier. Even if they thought their children could take advantage of a more extended secondary education, they could understand that they might not want to. 'I really left school before fifteen. I only went on about three days in my last year,' said one father. Some of the children were going to leave at Easter in the year they were

What the school asks of parents

sixteen. 'I'll really be glad when he *has* left - and he'll certainly be happier,' said another father about his son in the fifth year. The need for spending money was felt to justify her boy's dislike of the later years of school, by one mother. 'They should let them leave earlier and go to work to earn money. All boys smoke and if they can't earn money for cigarettes they are likely to steal it,' she said.

Another mother whose daughter had gone on to the sixth form still recognised the school's entitlement to require her daily presence, but she thought the pupils should have some discretion whether or not to go in, depending on what was available for them on particular days. 'I think it is stupid that at seventeen-and-a-half she has to take a note to teacher if she is away for a day. I know the school are in the right, but it's not treating them in a grown up way. She's used to it - you'll have to write a note, she says. She does take days off, but works at home. A lot of teachers are never there. There may be three people, but no teacher all the morning or all the afternoon. If they try to join another class they're told they can't go in. The teacher should be there, whether there's two or fifty-two. She minds if she takes all her books up for something special and it doesn't come off.'

This mother's attitude is in contrast with that of another mother, whose daughter was in the sixth form at another school. On one occasion her daughter took one or two days off unofficially, but the mother would not support her by writing a note. She felt the absence was unjustified, and to send a note would be 'collusion'.

Although the requirement for children to attend school that most parents acknowledged has national legislation as its basis, it was with the school rather than the education system that parents seemed to feel they had a kind of bargain to share the custody of their child. In a later discussion of parents' attitudes to agency workers (Chapter Seven) we shall see that although parents expected to notify the school if their children were away, and conversely expected the school to let them know if the child was playing truant, they were ready to be indignant about the intervention of the EWO, unless he was clearly acting as an intermediary for the school rather than the education office.

<u>Parents' attitudes to their children's homework.</u> Parents' attitudes towards homework and the part they should play here varied considerably. There was a marked difference in opinion about the need for homework and how much homework children should do. About a third of the parents we interviewed tended towards the view that children were expected to do quite enough work at school, and that their time at home should be their own. Such parents mostly admitted that they did not put

pressure on their children to do homework, and a few were almost disapproving of the amount of effort their children put into homework on their own initiative. The four schools had the policy of securing parents' agreement of the homework timetable, and this had given several parents the opportunity to signify they did not agree to the timetable. However, more than half the parents we saw accepted homework as part and parcel of school life and a few were critical of the casualness of homework arrangements. 'They ask them to do the homework and then they never seem to mark it.'

The role parents expected to play, apart from enforcing homework (or otherwise), was circumscribed by most parents' perception of the changing teaching methods and learning techniques since they themselves had been at school. This was mentioned most frequently in connection with maths. This may partly be because it is with maths homework that children most frequently turn for their parents' help, so that it is one school subject they were constantly coming up against. Some parents commented that when they were asked to help, they could do it in their own way and get the right answer, but this was no help to the child because they were using the wrong techniques. This was especially frustrating for some, because it was not that they felt they should do the child's homework, but that they should be able to help the child see how to do it.

With other subjects, the degree of help sought and offered was apparently less than this, although English was another subject frequently mentioned in the homework context. One or two mothers who prided themselves on English took particular care to read through essays and to correct misspelling. But, as many parents pointed out, the range of subjects presently being taught far outstripped the subjects they had learned at school and, more significantly, the standard achieved was much higher. Parents of older children often said they wanted to help, but now their child had progressed beyond their assistance.

The general picture was of parents trying to respond to their children's pleas for help, without interfering. They mostly felt less able to show the child the mistakes he or she was making than they might have liked. Again, despite the relatively little help they could offer, homework was another contact point with their children's increasingly sophisticated schooling, and at least an opportunity to see the books and the kind of work going on. And there did not appear to be a general difference between households in the amount of direct support parents felt able to offer. Even relatively well educated parents felt at a loss with modern teaching techniques. As one father put it, even his elder son who had only just left school could not help his younger daughter with her maths because things had changed so much even within that period of time.

What the school asks of parents

<u>Parents' attitudes to giving the school information about the family.</u> A great deal is made of the value of parent/teacher relationships as a preventive mechanism, which forestalls the development of crises, which helps the teacher understand the pupil and therefore teach better. For this to be effective, it was clear there had to be an information exchange and a sharing of knowledge of the child. Parents' views on the information the school would need to have, and how appropriate it was that they confide in the school, were an important element in any information exchange.

The majority of parents interviewed felt the school had a right to know about characteristics of the child's home background that might be felt to cause deterioration in school work. Their views differed about what these characteristics might be, and how the school would get to know. In contrast with these, there was a smaller number of parents who felt home and school matters should be separate and who, in effect, felt one not only should not impinge on the other, but that they were unlikely to do so.

It appeared that few parents had been approached for information about the family at the start of secondary schooling, and few could remember being asked to supply anything except emergency telephone numbers and information about exceptional health matters. Many parents supposed the records cards from primary school were passed on, and that schools told one another about special difficulties, an assumption which researchers' study of school records did not in fact confirm. Almost without exception parents conveyed a calm acceptance of the right for schools to use what information they had, and a willing disposition to be asked more, at least about the child and his or her interests.

Many parents felt the kind of information the school might need to know in the course of the child's secondary school life, would be to do with marital break-up or the death of a close relative, although a few could not think of the kinds of things that might affect school work sufficiently seriously to warrant them telling the school. So far as the possibility of emotional disturbances in adolescence was concerned, several parents observed that if teachers could not recognised and deal with this problem without being told by the parents, they were not much good as teachers. Some parents observed it would be superfluous for them to inform teachers of critical home events, since they found their children confided all kinds of private information to teachers.

This led to the question of what the parents themselves felt they had to tell the teachers. It appeared very few had taken the initiative to explain potential problems, despite a widespread opinion amongst those who had not had such difficulties to report that they would have told the school. Several schools, to our knowledge, had remained in ignorance of parents separating, and if they had got to know eventually, it was often by chance. One school had complained about the increasingly scruffy appearance of a boy, after which the father eventually told them his wife was no longer living at home. Some parents admitted to keeping a watchful eye on their children to see if family traumas were having an effect, stating that it they had detected a reaction they would have told the school about what was going on.

A few parents were confident that if the teachers noticed anything wrong, they would ask either the pupil or the parents direct. This demonstrated a remarkable faith in teachers' perceptions, which in some though not all cases was shown to be justified. One father remarked, without rancour, that he had been telephoned by a pastoral teacher who had heard that the parents were splitting up. Was this true? The father, while denying the rumour, seemed pleased that the teacher had bothered to make a check.

Some teachers have been reported as saying that they are having to deal with an increasing number of domestic problems, because parents have no one else to turn to. The evidence for our study was that there are far more domestic problems affecting the lives of pupils than are known about by teachers.

In addition to 'required' activities there were three topical issues about possible forms of parental support for school, about which parents expressed opinions - financial support, school government and decision making, and taking part in the school day. These will be briefly discussed before turning to some of the more informal and home-based forms of support for the school which parents described.

Parents' attitudes towards helping the school financially. The question of whether the parent should help out financially was one on which parents' views were divided. About half saw it as a natural extension of the parents' support for his or her child to make contributions to school funds, to send articles for jumble sales, to sponsor walks for fundraising and so on. They thought it reasonable to enhance existing provision to enrich not only their own child's school environment, but, by implication, all pupils. The number of parents subscribing in this way exceeded by far the number of parents who, through the PTA, were concerned with organisation of the event. These parents gave the lie to the view of the activists that those not actively concerned did not care about more than just their own child's school life.

Other parents, although they contributed from time to time, questioned how appropriate it was for parents to be expected to add to the school's resources. A common view here was that the local authority makes itself responsible for educational provision, and it should not be up to parents to make good any shortfall. Even some activists in the PTA felt this way, and to some extent their activity in the PTA could be seen as a willingness to join a pressure group to ensure the education authority properly fulfilled its duty.

Parents' views about their role in school government and educational decision making. This brings us to the issue of the parents role in decision making in educational affairs, a feature which became more at issue in the seventies than ever before. Did parents feel that teachers have an obligation to take notice of the parental point of view and did they feel they themselves had a right to express a view and to insist it was recognised? Parents challenged on this question responded thoughtfully, though for many it was obviously a novel perspective.

It was implicit in the actions of several parents that, when education issues had arisen concerning the teaching arrangements affecting their child, they had felt it appropriate to visit the school and put their own point of view. From several discussions about occasions of this sort it was evident that parents had expected account would be take of their views, although they recognised that the school might have counter arguments and reasons for their actions. Some had been satisfied with explanations of teacher shortage, and complications over pupil numbers and could sympathise with the school's problems. This experience over private matters was unconsciously paralleled in many parents' reactions to the possibility of parental influence in general educational affairs. Many said the parents had a right, some even said a duty, to put their point of view, and thought that the school had an obligation to listen. The school did not, however, have an obligation to accept the parents' suggestions, but many thought that there should be open discussion with the headteacher and staff so that parents could understand the constraints the staff were working under, or the educational arguments in favour of what the school proposed to do.

Parents were still of the view that education was the teachers' domain and most felt that for most of the time this could be safely left in their hands. A substantial minority of parents felt it inappropriate for parents to seek to intervene at whatever point, but this was sometimes at odds with what they told us they had said to teachers (for example, such parents had not necessarily felt inhibited from questioning teachers over arrangments for continuity in the teaching of maths). The view that working class parents had an exaggerated respect for the professionalism of teachers was not borne out in our study. In line with Shipman's observations (Shipman, 1968) that modern teaching techniques teachers out of the realm of obscurity, and more open to the view and opinion of parents, many parents obviously had an attitude towards teaching and were not afraid of criticising. Nevertheless, the idea of formally presenting an alternative case was uncongenial to most parents. It became apparent that even amongst parents who expressed interest in parent governors, few would find this role personally attractive.

So for many, the question of parental influence on the school was still confined to expressing a view about their own children and was unlikely to be exercised through institutional means such as parent associations or governing bodies. However, the notion of collective parental action and pressure occurred to many more than just those already involved in parents' associations. Some parents specifically mentioned a case concerning uniform at one school, when the arrangements whereby it could only be obtained through a central London store provoked many mothers to voicing their complaint. Others could hypothesize about certain kinds of school matters upon which the parents might have a common perspective and acknowledged parents' rights to join together in pressurising the school. Yet, often associated with these speculations, was the view that certain kinds of things were not the parents' domain. Problems such as uniform, school dinners, option choices were felt to be legitimately open to parental questioning, but more esoteric matters, such as teaching style or curriculum content were often cited as being matters for the professional judgment of teachers.

Although few parents realised that their own school governing body had provision for a parent governor, a number commented on this idea approvingly. There were concerns expressed about how representative such an individual could be, and one or two put forward the view that such an individual would only be able to take up issues that concerned him as a parent and not the general parental body. But for other parents, the idea of a lone representative parent on the governing body exactly reflected their view of how parents should interact with the school. That is, they felt the parent voice should be heard, but not necessarily heeded.

<u>Parents' attitudes towards participating in the school day.</u>
Finally, there is the question of the parents' involvement during the school day, which again was a novel suggestion to many parents of secondary school children, although some had encountered this arrangement in primary schools. Comments on possible contributions by parents were more concerned with what the school might gain than with the fact that such participation might improve home/school relations or educate parents about the school environment. The majority of parents came to the conclusion it was not appropriate to offer to help during the school day. This was principally because parents could not offer the skills relevant to secondary

schooling, but partly because the pupils themselves were thought to be likely to be more embarrassed. Another point often made was that few parents could help because they were working. One or two parents who knew of others who had listened to reading at secondary school level commented favourably on the idea of helping out, but the majority could not see what a parent could do and thought their influence would be disruptive.

There was however one area in which a number of parents, quite unprompted, concluded there might be benefit for parental contribution. In careers teaching, as we have noted before, many parents thought themselves as well if not better equipped to advise than teachers. Hence a few parents observed it might be a good idea for parents to contribute to careers sessions by giving talks on their own jobs. Nonetheless, these suggestions were hedged around reservations about the need to make sure this was not disruptive to the school day.

Parents' accounts of their home-based support for their children's education. Although contemporary educational issues such as school government and participation in the school day seemed to find little resonance in the experience and interest of the mothers and fathers interviewed, parents highlighted many ways in which they gave home-based support to their children's schooling. These varied from simple home-making to providing educational opportunities over and above those supplied by the school.

Not surprisingly many mothers stressed their home-making role. Several had deliberately delayed taking part-time or full-time jobs until they were satisfied their children were no longer dependent on finding them at home. 'I think it's important that there should be someone at home waiting for them, when they are small.' Some explicitly stated that their role was to send the child off to school well fed and properly dressed, and let the teachers get on with 'filling his head'. In harmony with the point made earlier about mothers' and fathers' roles in relation to the secondary school, some mothers were conscious that at this stage holding the home together was their major contribution, whilst the father's contribution was perhaps becoming more direct.

Discussions with the child about what went on during the school day were another aspect of family life which the majority of parents found kept them in important and valuable contact with their child's schooling. It was chiefly through informal chat with their children that they found out about different teachers, what subjects at school were like and what kinds of work the child was being expected to do. Parents valued these sessions and most thought they got fairly truthful accounts from their children about what they had been up to.

In some families the support provided by home-making and casual but interested enquiry was supplemented by a much more active interest in school work and what the family itself could do. One family made special trips to sites of geological interest, and were arranging their holiday venue around the son's interest in geology. This seemed in no sense an imposition on the family, who appeared to have gained a new field of interest from the son's studies.

Parents with individual criticisms of particular schools were also making plans for compensating their children for perceived inadequacies. Lack of specialist languages, lack of technical training and other deficiencies in the secondary school were considered to be corrigible by a year in a relevant technical college. Some parents, dissatisfied with the pattern of maths teaching, were themselves trying to put this right by teaching the children directly using old methods. We had the impression of a widespread resourcefulness amongst parents, even parents who were not themselves highly educated.

It should be noted that it is not only the parents who form the 'educogenous' aspect of family life. Parents were often highly dependent upon the advice and experience of older children who were about to leave or had recently left school, regarding decisions which had to be made on behalf of younger children still of compulsory school age. And there were many accounts of ways in which brothers and sisters helped their siblings to understand and cope with the pressures of school life.

Parents offered more active support in several other ways. Many parents bore witness to the demands they felt obliged to meet in terms of fetching and carrying children to and from certain types of school events, or to allow them to engage in special studies such as sport and music. Parents owning their own transport were obviously more involved here, and again it it true to say there was marked difference in the willingness of parents to put themselves out in this way. Some thought of it as a natural part of parenting, others that 'if the kids were keen enough, they would find their own way.'

There is little doubt that most parents considered the home should provide an appropriate and sympathetic backdrop to the child's school career. None of the parents seemed to be trying to set the child against the school, although there were a number of parents who were sceptical either about what the particular school was trying to do, or who were not impressed by the secondary schools' potential role in socialising their children. Of these, some particularly stated they would never devalue the school, nor criticise it in front of their children lest the children pick up this attitude themselves. 'I would always support the teacher's point of view, even if I privately disagreed,' 'I'd never belittle the teacher'.

However, in a few interviews the impression was conveyed of a family view that secondary schooling was a necessary stage which the child had to accept and live through, but which was of little value. Some of these parents were confident they could make up for the inadequacies of school life. One mother thought that parents provide a much more realistic and practical training. 'They've learnt more from me about what life is like. The teachers just aren't in touch with reality.'

Some of the parents never seen by the school were those who considered that the support they offered was through the security the home was designed to provide. It would be far from accurate to call these parents 'uninterested'. But their interest in their children's schooling was paralleled by an interest in their many other activities. One parent protested against its being said he took special interest in the children's schooling. 'As a parent you're interested in everything they do. School is only part of their life.' A number of parents were irritated by the seeming lack of recognition of this fact amongst teachers.

Among all the families we met there was reflection and speculation about the most proper role for parents which, for us, exposed the myth of the apathetic parent. The parents' view of their influence, about the maturity of their children and the child's own school career have been put forward as factors affecting whether the parent will be disposed to sustain a relationship with the school. These take us beyond any class analysis to a recognition of the importance of family dynamics and their influence on parental style. We are conscious these interview findings need testing out more rigorously, but are confident these factors are significant in an understanding of the relationships between parents and teachers. Their implications for the conduct of home/school liaison will be returned to in Chapter Eight. Meanwhile we turn to a consideration of those other institutions which may have a part to play in linking home and school – the welfare agencies.

Chapter Seven

HOME, SCHOOL AND THE WELFARE AGENCIES

There is a whole constellation of agencies, a substantial sector of whose clients are children of secondary school age - for example the school health service, the education welfare service, the school psychological service, the child guidance clinic, the youth and community service, the careers service and the juvenile bureau. Some of these services come within the education department of the local authority. Others are health authority services, and the juvenile bureau is part of the police authority. We have described the work of these agencies, and the contact they have with secondary schools, elsewhere. (Johnson et at, 1980) In this chapter we discuss parents' experience and knowledge about these agencies. One purpose of our enquiry about the contacts which families had with agencies was to ascertain to what extent the secondary school was seen as a means of access to the whole welfare network with which the schools have contact. A further purpose was to assess how successful welfare agencies might be in acting as intermediaries between home and school.

From our interviews with parents we formed the impression that they knew little about the specialist services available. With the exception of two or three families to whom more detailed reference will be made later, most parents offered no spontaneous examples of agencies they had made contact with through the school. When prompted more specifically, most parents had some comment to make about the school health service and the careers service, and most knew something about the work of the education welfare office (EWO), though few had ever met one. Thirty-six of the parents interviewed said that they had never had a call from an EWO (whether known by this title or as a School Board man) at any time during the children's school life. Yet children in several of these families had had episodes of truancy at some time during their school life.

The name of more specialised agencies, such as the school psychological service or the juvenile bureau of the police, seemed to mean little or nothing to the parents interviewed, nor was there any apparent consciousness of the possibility that access to social work help might be available through the school.

We cannot explore here the many reasons why families appear to have so little knowledge of the specialist agencies which augment or refine the broader social interventions of the maintained educational system, the national health service and the forces of law and order. A number of explanations have been lengthily debated elsewhere (see for example Titmuss, 1968; Pinker, 1971; Davies, 1978). Our concern in this chapter is to discuss such information as we were able to obtain about parents' school-mediated experience of agencies and consider the feasibility of the school's being seen as the channel for delivery of specialised agency services to families.

THE SCHOOL HEALTH SERVICE

The one service whose name and function all the parents recognised was the school health service. Checks on the health of school children have for many years been part and parcel of educational provision, and this arrangement persisted even after the setting up of the national health service in 1948. Most of the parents who talked to us about the school health service still seemed to see it as part of educational provision, and in some cases evaluated it as an alternative to the national health service and the national dental service, even though in 1974 responsibility for the service had been transferred to the health authorities, as a school-age-specific sector of the national health provision.

Only a very few parents felt the school health service to be redundant now that free health care was available to all. 'These services' (the school health service and the school dental service) 'are a waste of money', said one mother categorically. The weight of opinion, among those parents who talked about the school health service, was however in favour of its existence and continuance. One parent commented that even though medical treatment was free through the national health service at the present time, this might not always be so and then the school health service would be even more important than it was at present. Many of the parents made appreciative comments about the monitoring role of school health provision. "I think the school health service is a *must*", said one mother. "It is very good for picking up and drawing attention to things that may be going wrong." And her husband commented, "Even if we don't use the school health facilities, they can check, and we can carry out the necessary steps."

Even if parents felt that they themselves were unlikely

to overlook health problems in their children, it was several times pointed out that not all parents could be assumed to keep a close eye on the children's health. The proverbial 'other' parents who might be 'rather lax' could need the monitoring help of the school health service more than the parents being interviewed. But some parents considered that independent routine checks could be helpful for all families. Even concerned parents might find that the school health service could point out things that they were not aware of. And because all the pupils were given medicals, the children felt 'less singular' when they had to have their check up.

One or two parents thought the school health service was insufficiently rigorous. The medicals, though useful, were infrequent, brief and 'basic' these parents considered, although one such mother was appreciative that doctors did ask questions about behaviour at home and any parental worries about health.

Families whose initial introduction to the local clinic had been through the school health service sometimes continued to take their children to the clinic rather than to their GP because they had formed a more favourable opinion of the facilities available to them there. One mother found that going to the clinic was better than waiting at the doctor's surgery which was often crowded out. Moreover, the clinic doctor had more time available to attend to the child. Another mother found the clinic doctor more helpful than her own GP with regard to the children's health problems.

Medical inspections carried out at the school were theoretically at least a regular if infrequent point of contact between the school health service and all the families. However, many of the parents interviewed gave their signed permission for the medical to take place, but did not accept the invitation to be present when their child was examined at secondary school, though they said they had done so at primary school age. Usually it was the secondary school pupils themselves who had asked their parents not to come up for the medical, and most of the parents seemed to share their children's view that no useful purpose would be served by the parent being present. In some cases mothers felt their sons would be embarrassed by their presence at the medical examination.

Like many other happenings in secondary school life, the medical seems to be seen as an occasion when a child could be left to stand on his own feet and gain some experience in conducting his own affairs. But if the findings of the medical were other than routine, and a further appointment was offered, the parent might step back in the picture.

If parents did think it appropriate to be present at school medicals, it was almost invariably the mother who attended. In all the parent interviews only one father was referred to as having been present at a medical examination, although several fathers expressed a view as to whether such medicals were of value.

On the whole, the parents interviewed seemed to be fairly easy in their minds about their older children's health.[2] Certainly contagion as a bi-product of school-based education was not prominent in the thoughts which parents expressed about the health of their secondary school age children. For most families the contagious diseases of childhood are worked through during the primary school years. The only potential contagion which a few parents referred to was the possibility of hair infestation. References to the checking of hair cleanliness carried out at their children's school sometimes led to reminiscences about the parents' own school days – hair inspections seemed to be one element of school life which had not changed over the years.

For most of the parents it seemed that the school health service acted as a kind of preventive backstop for the protection already available through routine national health provision. It was not the role of the school to keep a close eye on the pupil's health, but the school did provide a convenient setting for the delivery of routine preventive measures such as vaccination and innoculation which could appropriately be carried out on an age group basis.

In most cases the GP was the family's obvious and primary link with medical care. Whereas in the primary school the health of the young child had been a frequent point of discussion between teacher and parent, the secondary school teacher did not seem to be seen as having a part to play in family oversight of the secondary school child's health. This was now a matter between the family and the medical profession. However one mother considered the school *should* take a closer interest in the pupil's health. At the secondary school stage the school, she felt, could well have more influence than the home on the young person. It was important that the school should be as fully informed about the child's health as about any aspect of the child's welfare, so that the influence exercised by the school could be congruent with any influence the home was trying to exert.

---

[2] Even so, quite a high proportion of the families interviewed made reference to the chronic health problems of one or another of their children, asthma and diabetes being the most frequently mentioned conditions.

EDUCATION WELFARE SERVICE

The service of education welfare is meant to provide one of the main liaison channels between school and home, and education office and home. Like the former school attendance officers, education welfare officers follow up cases of absence from school, maintain a register of children of school age living in the borough, and of transfers when school children for one reason or another go on and off school rolls. If a child moves out of the borough, the education welfare service notifies the receiving authority of the arrival of a school age child. These duties are all related to the compulsory nature of school attendance. But the education welfare service, as its name implies, has duties wider than attendance checking. Education welfare officers are able to advise parents about, and help them to make application for, a number of education-related benefits, including uniform grants and free school meals. Where appropriate, and particularly in cases of family crisis such as the death of a parents, EWOs will also refer families to the local social work team.

The working relationship between EWOs and the school they service varies widely, but in some circumstances the EWO will act as go-between for school and home, perhaps informing parents of the school's concern about a child's behaviour - not necessarily associated with non-attendance - and asking the parent to come to the school to talk the matter out.

The title of education welfare officer and its abbreviation, EWO, has been in use since 1944. However, only a handful of parents recognised the title, though many more referred to the school attendance man or the school board man (a name which has persisted more than seventy years after the dissolution of the School Boards which first administered maintained schools). One mother in her early thirties who did know the title EWO commented interestingly 'We call him the Bobby Green man - that's a very old name'.[3] Another mother, whose twin son and daughter, the youngest of a family of six, were now in the sixth form, had only just heard about the role of the education welfare officer through a talk she attended at the townswomen's guild.

For one or two parents, the mention of the word 'welfare', even in this education context, seemed to produce an immediate reaction of rejection. 'Education welfare - is that when you're a bit ... down, helping you?' asked one

---

[3] We have been unable to trace this expression in the various dictionaries we have consulted. Can any reader help?

father, looking rather embarrassed. They had always managed without such help. This family had six daughters, none of whom was yet of working age. And the mother of a family of eight said that the school did write about clothing grants and the EWO also explained and brought a form for a clothing grant application. 'But they want to know everything about you. My husband doesn't like that sort of thing. We've always managed up to now.' They had managed by the husband working double shifts, and the wife going to a cleaning job at 5.30 in the morning.

One or two parents wished they had known about the EWO in the past, but felt that most of the expenses associated with launching their children in secondary education were behind them, and they could manage all right now. "I've never heard of or seen the education welfare office. We could have done with him when we first moved here and couldn't afford the uniform - but we got through," commented one father.

Whilst parents had relatively little to say about the welfare element of the EWO's role, the question of attendance checking gave rise to much more discussion. One father, a shift worker on the railways, stated categorically that attendance enquiries were scarcely at all pursued in the area and those whose task it was to make these enquiries (the EWOs) evidently took their duties pretty lightly. "You can tell them from me - they've got a good job - they'd better keep it! There are children round here who are off all the time, and you never see anyone go to the door about it."

This father was making his judgment on the basis of what he perceived as the bad attendance records of neighbours' children. His own three children had been regular attenders at school. His wife, however, commented that the EWO had in fact called once at their own home, when one of the daughters was ill.

Cases of attendance checking calls made in error or felt by parents to be unjustified came up in several interviews. It is of course natural that such unnecessary calls should be remembered more readily than the unsurprising call made for good reason. Even though the incident had often taken place several years ago, some families' accounts were full of indignation at having been called on when the child's absence was justified, and the school already knew this. One family had had two such calls as the mother explained with some irritation - "My boy was off school with a broken leg and the school knew about it. But the School Board came round. I said 'I don't keep him at home for nothing - you can see him on the couch with his leg in plaster.' And in the infants, one of the children had chicken pox. I'd already sent a note to the school so I was annoyed when the man called round."

Failure by the school to make a note in the register of information received from the home was the reason for another inappropriate call by an EWO, this time on a family who were closely involved in parent/teacher activities at the secondary school. The mother commented, "The only row I've ever had with the school was when a welfare man came round to see if my eldest girl was truanting. The school already *knew* she'd been in hospital for five weeks with appendicitis, and they'd been asking after her. It was a genuine slip up." (The EWO had checked the registers without the help of the senior teacher responsible for them.) "But I was annoyed. So many children are *always* absent, but I have a job to get mine to stop off even when they're ill."

Other families however seemed to feel that truancy was always a possibility, even in the best regulated families. They were appreciative when a single, untypical absence had been followed up. Any move towards truancy by one of their children had, they felt, been nipped in the bud. One mother recalled 'a couple of wild moments' some fourteen years previously when her first child was five or six years old. He came home from infants school on two occasions and said he had the afternoon off. 'A school board man came round and took him back. He was a nice man - fatherly - but I was so taken aback! It shows they'll all try it on. He got the stick at school for that, and didn't do it again.'

In cases where truancy had become a problem in the families we encountered, parents sometimes built up quite a close working relationship with the EWO. One such mother had had three boys at secondary school, all of whom had been reluctant attenders. She tried, with the help of the EWO, to get her third boy into a special unit for persistent non-attenders which had been set up in the borough. But 'he didn't get it. Boys ten times worse than him got it - the school picked them out'.

The ability of the EWO to play the role of go-between for school and parent seemed to depend on the personality of the EWO and the length of time he or she had worked in the area. All of the comments which follow relate to the same EWO, who had lived and worked in the same locality for a number of years. One mother explained that her daughter's previously good work at school had been falling off, and she had been getting to school late. 'The EWO came down to see me, and asked me to see someone at the school about my daughter's lateness. It was helpful having the contact through him. He fetched my daughter's report to me and fixed for me to see the head lady teacher.' Another mother, who had three sons, said, 'Once my middle boy was away. The school board man rang up because he'd noticed that three boys in our Close were all away on the same day, and he thought that a bit funny.' Her boy's absence was for a genuine reason, but she felt it quite reasonable for the EWO to ring her when he explained. The anecdote told by yet another mother indicates how the EWO had built up his knowledge of children in the area over the time. 'Once my husband had a day off and he said the boys could have a day off and we'd all go fishing. But it poured with rain so we let the boys go on their own and arranged to pick them up. Then there was a bloke from the school' (the EWO) 'on the doorstep. He'd just seen them and he knew the eldest boy from school. My husband explained it was quite all right, we knew about it. I didn't mind the man coming, he was ever so nice, he said as long as *we* knew where they were. He gets to know the children at the school - he stops them if he sees them out and they don't mind.'

This parent's reference to the EWO as a 'bloke from the school' undoubtedly recognises the close link between this particular officer and the school he served. The school too valued this EWO. The service he offered was seen by teachers not as part of the work of an outside agency, but rather as part of the school's own pastoral work. Nevertheless EWOs are not on the staff of schools, but are employees of the education department of the local authority. In most cases parents correctly identified the attendance officer with the education office rather than the school, and they sometimes resented enquiry from that source which they would have considered acceptable if made directly by the school.

However, when absenteeism from school had become a perennial family characteristic, manifested by each child in turn, the EWO might become a more welcome resource to the family. 'Not everyone round here likes her' (the EWO) said one mother, 'but I do. I'd rather have her on the doorstep than the ruddy police.' All the children in the family were reluctant school attenders, and in trying to prevent them from truanting this mother felt that her working relationship was with the EWO rather than directly with the school. Mother and EWO worked in a kind of partnership to keep track on truants. At the time of the interview, the mother commented that the 'school board lady' had not been round for two weeks. 'I give her till 5 o'clock - she works till then. I tell the boys, I shall know if you've been wagging it - Mrs. P. will be round.' On one occasion the EWO had escorted the whole family to school. The relatively close relationship which this family had, not only with the EWO but with other agency practitioners, will be returned to at the end of this chapter, when we discuss the agency contacts of some families with a number of social problems.

Given that attendance-checking is still the most salient function of the education welfare service, and that most parents take for granted and cooperate with the requirement for their children to attend school regularly, it is not surprising that few of the parents interviewed seemed to see the school as the natural channel of access to the more specifically welfare aspects of the service of education welfare (or indeed, except for the few cases mentioned, to themselves and the school). Unless public perception of the role of the 'school board man' changes drastically, and unless the ratio of EWOs to school pupils is massively increased, only a minority of families will ever be in contact with this service, either directly or through the intervention of the school.[4]

THE CAREERS SERVICE

If any service exists for which the school might seem to be the obvious channel for universal access, it is the careers service. All the secondary school children are potentially, and in most cases fairly imminently, members of the working population. Parents with a child in the upper years of secondary school (fourth year and onwards) have already been supporting that child for fifteen years, including about ten years of compulsory schooling. It might be assumed that the careers service, mounted by the education department of the local authority, and statutorily available to all young people, would be well-known to parents, its function clearly understood and fairly consistently and positively evaluated.

In fact, parental knowledge of, expectations about and attitudes to the careers service varied extremely widely. Since only two branches of the service (one in each local authority) were being referred to, it must be assumed that most of the variation in knowledge, experience and attitude derived from the way in which access to the service was mediated by the four schools, or from the family's own ideas about moving into employment. A third possibility is of course that individual careers officers varied so widely in their job performance that parents were in fact encountering idiosyncratic versions of careers help. A small number of families did in fact distinguish between the careers officers their children had seen. 'The first one was no help at all. The second one really tried to do quite a lot.' But in most

---

[4] A substantial sector of opinion within the education welfare service favours the positive promotion of their role as that of school-based social workers, and the title EWO, still so little known to parents, has now been superseded by the name "education social worker". So far as the parents are concerned, our research seems to indicate that the EWO is already to some extent seen as an intrusive figure in the home and school contact about attendance, and if the social work responsibilities of the role are more prominently stressed the majority of families may feel the service has even less relevance for the school life of their child.

cases officers, in ways that implied fairly firm expectations or opinions on their own part, which had been either confirmed or repudiated by their experience of the service as a whole.

Perhaps the most influential factor was the assumption, widespread among the parents we interviewed, that getting a job was a question of self help - a task for the family, or for the school-leaver himself. Careers advice, from school or local authority, although very frequently referred to, whether favourably or unfavourably, was clearly seen *as* advice, or help, but not as directly instrumental in placing a school-leaver in work. Some parents explicitly absolved the school itself of any such responsibility. "I don't expect the school to get them a job." And few parents appeared to expect that officers of the careers service who saw the child at school or in the careers office, would actually find them employment.

An exception to this was the careers officer for the disabled. Here the expectation of one family undoubtedly was that after a physically handicapped boy had successfully completed the course of training recommended by this officer, a job where he could use his acquired skills would be found for him. The expectation was unfortunately ill-founded. "The disabled employment officer said they had nothing for him in the area - this was shattering for the boy", said his father. "They wanted to send him off again on a disablement resettlement course - but he said 'I'm not leaving home no more, I'm not going away again. I've been away from home nearly all my life.' I said, 'All right son.'"

This was the case of an older brother of one of the pupils whose parents we interviewed. In our interviews of parents with children currently attending comprehensive schools we came in contact with a few cases of other family members with particular handicaps, who in most cases had attended special schools. As an isolated case this disappointment on the part of the family of the handicapped boy cannot be seen in any sense as typical either of the achievements of a particular careers officer for the disabled or of the expectations of the parents of handicapped children. It does however point up the fact that the expectation of being placed in a particular job by a careers officer is a residual, last-ditch hope when the usual channels of family or individual self help have been exhausted or are for some reason ineffectual or inappropriate. In fact, happily, the boy in question did in due course succeed in finding himself a job. "He is not well paid - he has to have supplements at home, but he is living his own life. That's what we wanted for him," his father said.

Although most families seemed to see actual job-getting as a family matter, and to be looking only for careers advice, this was not the only reason why their perceptions of the careers service as such were rather shadowy. In some families, no distinction was made between careers advice available from the school - that is, actual teaching about job opportunities or advice and information available from the careers teacher on the school staff - and careers advice mediated by the school, but given by a careers officer, a member of the local authority's careers service. If the parents had not been present when a pupil was given a particular piece of advice or information, they were often not clear whether it had emanated from a careers teacher or a careers officer visiting the school. It may be that the filtering, censoring effect of pupil-conveyed information was taking place here, as on other occasions when parents' only knowledge of what was happening at school came via the children. Although not all pupils were regularly taught by the careers master or mistress, most would know whether or not the individual talking to them was a member of school staff or a visitor to the school.[5] Yet the distinction between the two did not seem to be similarly clear to their parents.

In cases where the advice given had been unexpected, influential, or in conflict with the pre-formulated aims of child or family, however, parents usually had a clear idea who had offered the advice in question. A number of parents with children at one of the schools spontaneously, explicitly and unfavourably assessed the competence of the careers teacher as biased, ill-informed and unimaginative. They felt this individual to be intellectually and temperamentally unsuited to a careers teacher's task. Children were not allowed to express a range of choices, and the teacher did not try to fit the job to the aptitude of the child. Advice was limited to routine jobs and was perceived as sexist, in that certain jobs were labelled 'not a good job for a girl'. These parents said they did not expect the school to find a job for the child, but much more could be done by way of careers guidance.

In another of the schools where a careers teacher was individually identified and referred to by a number of parents opinions were more mixed, comments about the teacher being 'quite interested' and seeming to 'know what he was talking about' contrasting with other judgments that he 'wasn't up on his job at all'. One mother recognised that what the teacher could achieve depended to some extent on the pupil's response. While the careers teacher had never seemed very helpful, nor was her son very keen to get a job, at the end of his secondary school years. 'He doesn't like new things -- he's a

---

[5] Indeed the pupils interviewed during fieldwork in the schools concerned clearly differentiated between help offered by careers teachers and the interviews they had with visiting careers officers. (Johnson et al, 1980)

bit shy.'

More real family upsets about children's career aims or hopes seemed however to be generated by interviews with careers officers, not known by name to the children or parents concerned, but clearly identified as being from the careers office. Sometimes parents felt impotent to undo the effects of a careers interview which in their view had been damaging to a child's motivation for suitable and attainable work. One boy had been set on going into a bank. He had written the literature they sent him. In a subsequent careers interview (at which his mother was present) the boy was cross-questioned by a careers officer on the basis for his career intention. To the dismay of his parents he then decided to give up the idea of going into a bank. They were left with the feeling that the interview had done more harm than good.

In cases where the careers officer's advice conflicted with expectations the child appeared to have been encouraged in by the school, parents usually took the matter up themselves. A central discussion point of one home interview was the disappointment experienced by a seventeen-year-old girl who had followed the school's advice about exams and subject qualifications with a view to fulfilling her longstanding ambition to go on to the airport school, to train initially as a ground hostess. Then, in an interview with the careers officer, she learned that she had not after all been following the right courses. She would not be eligible to apply to the airport school. The parents verified this by writing to the airport, and then approached the school, expressing their willingness to pay if necessary for their daughter to follow the necessary extra courses. But it was too late. Her mother commented that they would not now allow their younger daughter's hopes to be raised by encouraging her in a particular ambition.

From an overall appraisal of the comments of a hundred parents about their general hopes and expectations of careers help by or through the school, it is tempting to conclude that the careers adviser, whether teacher or officer, cannot win. In many cases the advice is seen as irrelevant or unnecessary, since the family themselves are best fitted to guide the child into work. (This was the view expressed by the majority of the families contacted.) Or if advice *is* felt to be desirable, parental expectations about such advice may be diametrically opposed in different families. The word 'channel' was often used by parents when discussing careers advice, but it had varying connotations. One parent deplored the tendency of careers advisers to channel young people into particular kinds of work, while another family were pleased that their son had received advice which seemed to channel his aptitude and flair for art into an area of practical work. A similar view to this was expressed by a father of four who had hopes that by working with the children the school might 'fathom down to what they *could* be good at'. He would like to 'see them come out with some sort of *idea* of a trade – not necessarily being taught it there, but with their study and ideas programmed *towards* it',

The vehemence of comment about careers advice seemed to increase in intensity when we talked to parents with children in the fifth and sixth forms. From our study of all the interviews we conclude that this is not so much because parents of older children had more direct experience of careers advice from school or office – after all, many of the parents of children in the lower forms had gone through the careers advice process already with older children no longer at school. Rather it seemed to be a build up of family anxiety as the child now completing school moved closer to the moment of status passage from schoolchild to worker or student.

This was especially the case if the child's expectations and hopes seemed to be leading them in a direction outside of previous family experience. If the pressure to 'branch out' had not come from the family, those who seemed to have contributed to it – whether careers teachers or careers officers – were felt to be the bearers of much responsibility. If their advice was perceived as ill-founded or ineffective, parental anxiety was sometimes unleashed in heartfelt diatribes against them. Many of the parents interviewed undoubtedly gained considerable relief from 'letting off steam' to the interviewers regarding their uncertainties about their children's future. Whilst the catalyst for their outpourings was the question of careers advice, this often seemed only to be the presenting focus for uncertainties about more long-felt and negotiated changes in the parent/child relationship, especially if the child seemed to be moving beyond the well-tried areas of family experience of employment or education.

Feelings seemed to run particularly high with parents of sixth-formers, and it was of course the case that most of these young people were 'first generation' sixth formers. Most parents had left school at fourteen or fifteen. Few had experience of school leaving examinations, let alone of 'stopping on' for further study. While most were eager for their children to do well, and offered them such encouragement as they could, they were often keeping to themselves doubts about whether this further work would be 'any use', and these anxieties came out in interview, often in the form of criticism of those to whom their children now seemed to be looking for advice.

One girl in the upper sixth was felt by her mother to have been over-persuaded to take up art. "I don't say her artwork *isn't* creative, but she has got to be guided and told. Is she going to be able to teach art freely and happily? ... The school have encouraged her and the teachers have been quite helpful ... but if she can't get into college, two years will have been wasted."

For another family it had seemed best for their son to leave school and take up the opportunity of an apprenticeship which was offered after he had entered the lower sixth. Although his teachers disapproved, his parents persisted in withdrawing him from school. "We couldn't guarantee that he'd learn anything during that year which would help him to get a job." More recently, their youngest daughter had done exceptionally well in the sixth form, and had been offered a place at university. 'I've been to one or two careers meeting', said her father, 'but they were a waste of time. They didn't tell us anything or ask us anything -- no information, no advice, no help at all -- just "leave school and go on to university".'

A West Indian mother whose daughter was also in the sixth form said that she and her husband had got to the point where they accepted what the school said about their children's potential, but they did not always agree with or believe in it. 'If we were in our own country we might get more involved with the teachers — you would be able to talk to them as a person. But here we just accept what they say. I don't think they want us to become more involved.'

The first generation sixth-former is the focus of much parental attention and some bewilderment. Even the father who had himself attended a grammar school was not disposed to see sixth form work as automatically beneficial. 'I think my son has stayed on another year to put off the decision about what to do next -- certainly not for academic reasons. I have told him very strongly that whatever happens he's not stopping on *another year* -- as I feel sure he is just using it as an opportunity to mark time.'

There is room for considerable systematic research into the implications for family dynamics of extended secondary education.

THE SCHOOL AS A MEDIATOR OF WELFARE SERVICES

The idea of the schools, which cater for all children, as an appropriate channel of access to the welfare services which cater for families with particular needs, has been chiefly promoted by Fitzherbert (Fitzherbert, 1977). She postulates that the schools are well placed both to inform families about the services available to them, and also to put them in touch with those services.

Our own interviews with parents do not confirm that the schools their children attended played a mediating role of this kind. Although a number of families saw a functional link between the schools and the school health careers services, they were on most occasions likely to seek medical help or employment opportunities for their children some other way than through the school. The education welfare service, which could have provided financial and advisory help to families in need, was largely unknown to the parents interviewed except in its attendance chasing role. Even less did the majority of parents seem to be aware that the school could make referrals to social work teams or, through the school psychological service, to child guidance clinics.

Two mentions were made of referral to child guidance through family doctors, while a child was still at primary school stage, but only one family had taken their child to the child guidance clinic at the instigation of the secondary school, and one at the suggestion of a primary school headteacher. For many of the parents (and some of the teachers) there seemed to be an atmosphere of unease surrounding the words 'child guidance'. In the rare cases where the possibility of referral had been raised by teacher or parent the conclusion had usually been reached that referral was inappropriate as 'things are not so bad as *that*'.

Is it perhaps the case that the stigmatising qualities of agency help are such that parents are simply not prepared to reveal what referrals the school has made to social work or other agencies on their behalf? We cannot tell whether this is so. However, a study of the accounts which some families with multiple problems gave us of their dealings with agencies lead us to conclude that the school was not a mediating or central protagonist in their contacts with agency practitioners. Six such families were encountered during the research. A brief account of their circumstances will give some background to the attitudes to agency help which they expressed.

Two of the families had four children, a further two had five and the remaining families were of eight children. In each case at least one family member had health problems, and in most cases several instances were referred to of mental and/or physical illness of a fairly serious nature of several members of the nuclear or extended family. All appeared to be of limited economic means. In all cases one or both parents were in employment, in most cases working long or unsocial hours. In four of the six families, the hours of work of husband and wife were completely different from one another. At least two children in each family were currently at the schools researched; four of the families had other children at primary school, and two had had children at special schools.

One family's problems were solely (and seriously) those of health. The two children currently at secondary school were both achieving well, and seen as the 'best assets' of their evidently loving parents. This family's attitude to school as mediator of welfare will be discussed separately from that of the other families with problems. However, it is of interest to note that this family (whom we will call the

Merediths), like the other five families, did not wish to involve the schools in their arrangements for bringing up their children.

In the other five cases, the families' problems were a mixture of ill health (ranging from enuresis to paralysis) and conflicts with the law (ranging from truancy and domestic theft to housebreaking and assault). Their route of access to social work support and welfare help of various kinds had been either through the medical profession of the courts or both. Some of the children in each of these families had been in difficulty at school as well as in trouble outside it. Two sets of parents were at their wits' end to know how to deal with at least one of their adolescent children. But they seemed to have no thought of involving the school in their attempts to get help. One family had asked both the 'welfare' and the police to take the adolescent in question off their hands, but were told that no sufficiently spectacular criminal offence had yet occurred to make this appropriate. The child's earlier career in school had not been such as to encourage the parents to look for help in that direction. And in another family, a father whose son was stealing money from him, had no intention of bringing the school into the matter -- the boy was already in trouble of a different kind at school.

Most of these families were aware that their family name had certain associations in the minds of teachers. 'I think they think "Here comes another of them",' said one mother. Well aware of their children's failings, and also of their good qualities, parents were keen to make sure that school disapproval and punishment was only meted out when it was merited and not merely because of some generally unfavourable image presented by the family. It was in getting square with a teacher he claimed had struck his child unjustly that one father became involved in the assault for which he was subsequently convicted.

Yet, despite his violence, this father and all the other parents with family problems, had a respect for the educational function of the school, and a disposition to declare that teachers know best about teaching. But these parents - and the Merediths too -- wanted to restrict the sphere of the school in their lives, and certainly did not wish to extend its interest to any other of their family problems in which the school was not already perforce involved.

The idea of the school as an intermediary between family and social help presupposes a longstanding and comfortable relationship which encourages the revelation and discussion of what may be disturbing, embarrassing or unhappy circumstances. Our experience does not suggest that families with urgent welfare needs usually have such a comfortable relationship with their children's schools - and particularly not with their secondary schools, at a time when the young people are markedly more hard to handle than in earlier years.

All the parents of the five families now under discussion had frequently to go to the school in response to complaints about their children's behaviour. They had no propensity (and in most cases no energy) to go to the school for other purposes. One parent pointed out there was little incentive to make additional visit, providing a further opportunity to be told about one's children's wellknown defects, and how one was responsible for them. And if there were further skeletons in the family cupboard it was best to leave them there -- not tell the school about them. 'It would not enter my head to turn to the school for advice', this parent said firmly.

One mother did use the school as a means of access to welfare assistance and professional advice. She also made similar use of the health service, the legal system, her neighbours and any other opportunity that came her way, including the research interview. She had exercised her parental responsibilities by recruiting whatever help she could to ensure family survival. This mother, unlike most of the other parents with problems, was alertly opportunist rather than resignedly enduring or self-defeatingly aggressive in her coping strategies. But she would have regarded it as naive to make the school the chief or only channel for her procurement of money, goods or moral support. Nor did her children intend that she should become too closely involved with their school. "I go to lots of jumble sales, but not to the one at the school - the kids won't tell me when it it." she said.

Even this mother, who could see the practical advantages of maintaining close contact with the school, did not make the headteacher or the school counsellor her confidant. She negotiated with the school for help on matters the school already knew about, and kept less public problems for discussion with other professionals, such as 'the bloke from the welfare' or the legal aid solicitor. Like other parents she saw the school's main job as getting on with the business of teaching.

Children's experience of school, and their reputation with teachers, is obviously an important element in whether parents see the school as an appropriate way through to agency help. If some or all of the children are notoriously unsuccessful or troublesome at school, the parents are unlikely to have a sufficiently relaxed attitude towards school staff to be able to unburden themselves of difficult and distressing problems, and their own need for help.

But what of a family like to Merediths, whose children were valued and attractive members of the pupil population at the school they attended? Might not the Meredith's find school an appropriate means of access to the welfare help they sometimes badly needed? Apparently not. They too were determined to restrict the home/school relationship to purely educational matters. For one thing, the mutual confidence between parents and children might be impaired if the school became embroiled in every difficulty - "They know we won't go running up the school as soon as they tell us something - we sort it out together". And the children's life at school was a time when they could feel unencumbered and successful - not to be encroached upon by family griefs and burdens. Their father was adamant about this. "Anything we have to cope with at home should not affect their schooling - we've kept them going to school whatever happened. Unless it is affecting the child - that reason alone - we feel the school have enough of their own troubles, without bothering them with out troubles."

Most of the families we interviewed were faced with only run-of-the-mill problems of an unexceptional kind. It is from these average families' viewpoint that the home/school relationship is chiefly discussed in this book. For families in adversity - of varying and sometimes multiple kinds - the school has a value in offering a respite for the children from home problems and at least an opportunity to acquire competencies, but it does not seem to stand as an open gateway to agency help. Nor does it seem that the agency practitioners who contact families at home are often used as a bridge between home and school.

Part III

Summary and reflections

Chapter Eight

FAMILY AND SECONDARY SCHOOL - THE RELATIONSHIP RE-ASSESSED

This book has given a voice to the views and feelings of some parents about their children's secondary school years. The typicality of their views, and the factual accuracy of the family and school experiences on which their feelings are grounded should not be taken for granted. Some of the reservations which must be borne in mind about interview material and its interpretation by researchers are discussed in the appendix. But the insights which these research data give into what the idea of a home/school relationship may look like from outside the school cannot be ignored. In this chapter we shall reiterate what we believe to be the "messages" of our research with parents - messages which were briefly heralded in chapter one. And we shall consider what may be the potential of a relationship between home and secondary school as new cohorts of children live out their school days in the 1980s.

The principal insights arising from the research have, we believe, been: that parents and teachers have different views on the benefits of a home/school relationship; that teachers' expectations derive from primary school models of parent/teacher contact involving the dependency of the child, and that teachers evaluate parental support for the secondary school by the extent to which they visit the school.

To take first the question of how the success of home/school cooperation is assessed by teachers, it was evident from the literature reviewed in chapter two, and also from the research discussions with teachers, that the most accessible criterion is the readiness of parents to come to the school. Yet parents' accounts of the backing they gave to their children's secondary education included many home-based forms of support and interest which were unseen by teachers. And the reasons which prevented many parents from visiting the school were not solely those of apathy or conflicting priorities. Many parents positively took the view that it was better not to intervene in the developing relationship between the pupil and his secondary school. The child was learning to stand on his own two feet, and the teacher was bringing his professional skills to bear on the child's development. Unless something was going seriously wrong, the appearance of parents on the school scene might disrupt rather than help.

The teacher's definition of the cooperative parent as the visible accessible parent is linked with the assumption that cooperation between secondary school teacher and parent is potentially similar to cooperation between primary school teacher and parent. Essentially, the basis for cooperation is the perceived dependency of the child, and the need for adults around the child to work together for his benefit. Yet we have seen that, from the parents' point of view, many of the benefits which may be gained from personal acquaintance and contact with the child's primary school teacher cease to operate when the secondary school years are reached. Teaching has moved beyond the basic skills of reading, writing and counting, progress in which the lay adult can readily appraise, and feel able to assist. Secondary school subjects are perceived as specialised and constantly updated by new knowledge and teaching methods. If the child can cope with them, well and good. If not, no amount of contact between teacher and parent is likely to help.

Nor is the child's health any longer a non-controversial subject of contact between parent and secondary school teacher, as it may well have been during the primary school years. With the onset of puberty the adolescent's demands for physical privacy make him main custodian of his own health. If parents or teacher see cause for concern, they may try to persuade their son and daughter to accept advice or treatment, but to go over the adolescent's head and debate his physical problems and practices with another non-medical adult is rarely seen as appropriate. For the parent, the relevant professional is now the doctor rather than the teacher.

Sometimes, the contact between home and primary school has been particularly close. Parents have found a part to play in the day to day life of the school, or have gained personal enjoyment from the witnessing of children's display activities. Or, because of their child's initial reluctance to go to school, parents may have come alongside him at every opportunity, to give a sense of security and encouragement and share with his teacher in the allaying of his fears. With the move to secondary school, parents often review their own behaviour and attitudes. This is the time to make a break, or to step up the phased withdrawal which has been taking place over the early school years. The perspective now is forward to employment and independence rather than backward to pre-school years and dependency. From now on, the role of the parent in relation to the schoolchild becomes a more self-effacing one, so far as the provision of security is concerned, but also perhaps a more coercive one in terms of making progress towards economic independence. Neither development is obviously served by being hand-in-glove with the teacher (although a new role may be perceived for the teacher to which we shall presently turn).

These themes about the parent's perspective on the school, together with the folk-dance of relationships within the family, which bring parents and child now closer together, now further apart, have seemed to us to underlie much of what parents had to say about the secondary school years.

What are the present forms of home/school contact actually achieving?

Analytic and descriptive literature about the partnership between family and school, written from the point of view of the educationalist, has in the past pursued three main themes: the question of welfare, the question of values, the question of accountability.[6] Practising teachers, busy with the year-to-year pursuit of their craft, tend to give emphasis to the definition of home school relations which prevailed at the time they received their training. In the case of teachers contacted during our research, this was chiefly the theme of values - how familial attitudes might promote or hinder the educational progress of the child. This preoccupation found voice in an expressed desire to learn more about the home, to educate the parents about the benefits of secondary schooling, and to motivate parents to give more support in the schooling of their child. In the schools concerned, the actual opportunities for home/school contact were similarly ossified around the practice of the 1960s, taking the form of parents' evenings, PTA activity chiefly of the fundraising kind, and publicly accessible functions at the school. And teachers' debates about the objectives of the home/school relationship made little attempt to evaluate what home/school contacts, as currently organised, were actually achieving.

No doubt there are many secondary schools where policy and practice in the development and maintenance of a relationship between home and school is constantly updated and adapted to take account of new ideas and test the benefit of new forms of contact. But we are equally sure that there are many secondary schools like the four we studied during the latter part of the 1970s where, after the upheaval of reorganisation on comprehensive lines, the schools were, not unnaturally concerned to build on routine and regularity, rather than pursue innovation or critically monitor the outcomes of present practice.

---

[6]See Johnson, D. "Home-School Relations, 1970-1980" in Cohen, L., Manion, L. and Thomas, J., *Educational Research and Development in Great Britain*, NFER/Nelson 1982.

Family and secondary school

We have seen that in the schools studied, the most prominent opportunity for contact between home and school was at the parents' evening. These evenings, it seemed to us, fell far short of meeting the teachers' objective of getting to know the parents and the child's home background, and hence understand the child better. The public and bustling nature of the evenings was hardly conducive to the development of an acquaintanceship between teacher and parent, let alone to the developing appreciation by the teacher of the pattern and preoccupations of family life in the pupil's home, and how these impinged on his schooling.

We have already discussed at some length the many reasons why parents did not make frequent contact with their child's secondary school. But when they did make contact, what were they hoping for?

Broadly, it can be said that, compared with teachers, parents were expecting more from home/school contacts, but accepting less. They seemed to look to the parent/teacher relationship (a more personalised concept than that of a 'home/school' relationship) to enable mutual help in the handling of their particular child. It is in this sense that they expected more than the teachers did. They acknowledged that both parties had work to do for the child, for which they were variously equipped. And they anticipated that the teacher's professional knowledge of children could be applied to their own child in such a way as to offer expert enlightenment about his individual capacity and potential. As the child moved up the school, the question of what he would do after leaving school became increasingly central for parents. But all the way through parents were aware that their child was developing and changing, and they seemed to look to the teacher to give them clues about what they could anticipate from the child in the years ahead.

A pattern of home/school relations chiefly structured around parents' evening at the school did not match with parents' expectations any more than with teachers' objectives for the encounter. Nevertheless, the parents' evening seemed to some extent appropriate for what parents had in mind, and this may be why most parents essayed the encounter at least once. Ritually the occasion met the desire of parents to see the teacher face to face, to talk about their particular child. But aside from the fact that the meeting took place while other parents were nearby, with both teacher and parent under pressure to be brief out of consideration for the needs of others, the actual focus of discussion might not be what parents had in mind. Their orientation was towards the child's future, while the teacher proposed to review the successes and failures of the child's immediate past. This was what the teacher knew about and had prepared himself to discuss, in a marathon of retrospection about each of his pupils in a particular class over the past year. Small wonder that his comments of guidance for the child's future were usually confined to advice about remedying past error. "He'll need to pull his socks up, and apply himself more, if he's going to get anywhere." If there had been no noticeable past error, the teacher might have little to offer, from his exercise in retrospection. Hence the comment "Nothing wrong there" to the parents of an unobtrusive child, or the would-be complimentary but irritating comment, "You're not the ones we want to see" to the parents of a successful child.

In such encounters, the parents' hopeful expectation of psychologically based and expert assessment of the implications and possibilities of their child's skills and behaviour dies the death, perhaps never to be resurrected. Some parents accept the teacher's definition of the purpose of the occasion, and conclude that if there is 'nothing wrong', there is no need to go to the parents' evening; others conclude that if there is something wrong they are not going to get any help during such a brief and crowded encounter. Not a few parents continue to make a ritual appearance every year, but recognise that is is for the most part a ritual event, at which they and the teachers can find little to say to one another, but can 'talk about the weather'.

The parents' objective of picking the teachers' brains about their particular child can however more readily be achieved if the parents make an approach to the school as individuals. Many schools, including those studied, make every attempt to respond to parents' requests for ad hoc interviews. But the very fact that such encounters are by definition not institutionalised and 'laid on' means that parental initiative is needed to bring them about.

Some parents can only bring themselves to approach the school when they have built up a head of steam about some grievance, and are determined to 'have things out'. Unaccustomed to taking the initiative in social or business encounters, a number of parents gave us vivid accounts of how they had surprised themselves by tackling a teacher in a blustering and aggressive fashion quite unlike their usual demeanour. Such an approach must have been counter-productive to the parents' real aim of sorting things out, and if a high-handed approach triggered an equally high-handed response, it is not surprising that in at least one case teacher and parent came to blows. In their calmer moments, however, diffident parents were well aware of the teachers' wide ranging tasks and responsibilities, and expressed themselves as reluctant to 'trouble' the school about matters which people with a more activist outlook on life would have taken up without delay.

<u>What pattern of contacts would best meet the varying objectives of teachers and parents for a home/school relationship?</u>
One answer might be a home-based rather than a school-based encounter, in fact a visit by the teacher to the pupil's home. If teachers really want to get to know the parents and appreciate the child's home circumstances what better way to do so than by visiting the home? And if parents want the teacher to give thoughtful consideration to their child's future, would not the teacher's attention be more appropriately focussed in the child's home rather than in the school?

The objections to home visiting are manifold and well-rehearsed by teachers. To the outsider, some seem less well-founded than others. Given the stated aspirations of the schools we studied to foster home/school relations, it was perhaps surprising that home visiting by teachers was frowned on as a matter of policy. It was suggested that by calling on parents at home teachers would be exceeding their responsibilities, invading parents privacy, and probably laying themselves open to circumstances with which they were not equipped to cope. A senior teachers with wide experience of families with problems commented specifically that the young middle class female teacher would be clay in the hands of the manipulative parent, alert to gleaning personal advantage.

Whether teachers would in fact be exceeding their responsibilities in visiting the home seems open to debate. If parents and teachers are to some extent partners in child rearing, during the school-age years, with alternating responsibility for the child at different times of day, there seems no obvious reason why it is more appropriate for teacher and parent to consult together at the school rather than in the home.

At the school however the parent sees the teacher in his place of employment (although, for the most part, outside his 'working hours'). But the home is a private domain, and access to it must always be individually negotiated. The contention that home visits would constitute an invasion of privacy is therefore, perhaps, tenable in principle. But principles are not necessarily confirmed by practice. Parents we interviewed had, in a few cases, been called on by teachers, and without exception these occasions were mentioned appreciatively. Whether the teacher had called to bring homework for a sick child, to escort a child home from an outing, or (despite school policy) to discuss a problem of the child's attendance, behaviour or achievement, parents in spontaneously mentioning these events expressed their pleasure that the teacher had 'taken the trouble' to come round.

Another slender indication from our data of likely parental approval for home visits came from those parents who had recently immigrated to this country. Asian and West Indian parents alike had experience from their own childhood of teachers visiting the home, sometimes to lay down the law in no uncertain terms about how the child should mend his ways at school. They were surprised that teachers in Britain did not make similar approaches, and seemed to take for granted a closely shared evaluation by teacher and parent of the child's best interests.

Although only a few parents had actually been visited by teachers, some few more had been contacted at home by some other emissary from the school, from an education welfare officer offering to arrange a meeting between the parent and the concerned senior teacher, to a representative from the parent/teachers association rounding up support for functions at the school. Diffident, retiring mothers (who in our experience greatly outnumber the scheming, manipulative mothers referred to by the senior teacher) were particularly grateful for the encouragement and moral support which such approaches offered. One mother had never been contacted in this way, but wished that she had. If someone were to get in touch with her about events at the school and offer to meet her on the corner so she did not have to walk into the meeting on her own, it would make all the difference, she felt.

The welcome given to researchers calling to conduct home interviews is also relevant here. Although it was stressed that researchers were not *from* the school, but calling with the school's agreement and approval, parents frequently imputed a liaison role to the researcher, looking to us to explain the school to them and them to the school.

There is, we suggest, no doubt that considerable scope exists for strengthening home/school understanding by making some arrangement for parents to be individually contacted, from time to time, in their homes. But does all this imply that teachers should make regular home visits?

In fact the most practical and fundamental objection to such a proposal has not yet been raised, and was not put forward by teachers collaborating in the research. No teacher roundly stated that to undertake home visits as a matter of regular practice would be far too much work for teachers to undertake. The school policy of discouraging home visits perhaps freed teachers from the necessity of articulating this objection, but it is an entirely valid one. The thousand or so pupils in a comprehensive school come up from perhaps 800 homes. The 80 teachers who make up the staff of such a school might, without too much difficulty, visit ten homes each in the course of a year. But not all the 80 members of staff would be appropriate callers, if the purpose was to discuss with parents their particular child. Some specialist teachers know only a restricted group of children who take their subject. Other teachers have wide-ranging administrative responsibilities, but little classroom contact with pupils, while yet others have overall pastoral and disciplinary responsibilities for a sizeable section of the pupil populating, but close acquaintance with only a few children, exceptional in some way or another.

Moreover, even if teachers did each undertake to visit a number of pupils' homes, this could not render parents' evenings superfluous, since on the latter occasions parents can speak, however briefly and superficially, to a number of teachers each of whom has some intermittent contact with their child. So the teachers, in undertaking home visits, would be taking on an additional task rather than replacing the evenings spent talking to parents at the school with time spent in pupils' homes.

This brief exercise in head counting does however indicate that if schools were to have a policy of arranging for some teachers to make occasional home visits, perhaps twice in the pupil's school life, this might not be quite so impossible to carry out in practice as would at first sight appear. Some schools do have such a policy, and however rare the visits they do obviate the continuing anonymity of parents. In the schools we studied there were parents who, although they had four or five children attending the school over a period of ten or twelve years, were as unknown to the teachers as the parents of any first born to attend the school.

This book is not an account of research on the scientific model, where a high degree of objectivity and detachment is incumbent on the researcher. Within the constraints of time and our own capacity for understanding, our aim was to enter as fully as possible into the eye-view of those researched. In an earlier work (Johnson et al 1980) we have described and reflected on the teacher's eye view of the comprehensive school and its external relations with other groups and institutions involved with the secondary school child. In this book we have adopted the perspective of the parent, and discussed the schools and their children's secondary school years from the parents' point of view. In conclusion, we sum up by giving our own views on the potential for an appropriate relationship between home and secondary school, in the light of our research as a whole.

It seems to us that both teachers and parents are some degree mesmerised by the conventional wisdom and rhetoric of the campaign for closer relations between home and school which has been uncritically espoused for the past 20 years.

Even so, parents are perhaps more realistic than teachers in what they look for from the relationship between home and school. Parents recognise that such a relationship may have to meet different needs at different times during their of the relationship between home and school, because the child is the only reason for home and school to be involved together. As the child changes so the needs which a home/school relationship might meet will change. Teachers, on the other hand, can theorise about and make administrative arrangements for home/school contacts without having particular children in mind. Understandably, they sometimes see "parents" as a *body* of people, a client group, rather than the mothers and fathers of Tom, Dick and Harriet.

But although we consider parents' ideas about the home/school relationship to be more flexible and down to earth than those of teachers, we concede that many parents are unrealistic in what they expect to get from talking with teachers about their child. Whatever the circumstances of the parent/teacher encounter, whether at crowded parents' evening or during a visit to the home, the teacher cannot offer a psychological assessment of each child's emotional, intellectual and vocational capacity. What the teachers can fruitfully tell the parents, however, is 'this is how your child gets on in the institutional context of the school'. This is valuable information for parents to have, as a supplement to their own longer term knowledge of the child in the context of the family. Nevertheless, there may come a stage at which parents decide to do without that information, in recognition of the young person's growing autonomy and independence. When the school-leaver goes to work, he will have to learn to get on in the new environment without benefit of consultations between parents and employer as to his progress. For some young people the final years at secondary school provide a sheltered workshop for trying out the role of independent adult.

This developmental aspect of the secondary school years seems to be overlooked in the home/school literature, and indeed in the administrative arrangements made for parents to visit the school. Whatever arrangements are made for parent/teacher contacts at particular schools tend to be consistent throughout the secondary school years. These arrangements do not take account of the growing maturation of young people during their time at school.

The wisest parents, we contend, are those who are most sensitive to the phases the child is going through, in handling their own relationship with the school. The child is in any case an unheralded third party to the parent/teacher encounter in that, with very few exceptions, parents subsequently tell the child what has been said. Increasingly, as the child gets older, the relationship is appropriately a three-way one in which the child must figure. Eventually the pupil himself becomes unequivocally the teacher's client. The parent, still the legal guardian, must still be called upon for specific authorisation and confirmation of plans agreed between teacher and pupil. But parents are no longer part and parcel of the school's dealings with the child, as they were in earlier years.

Adolescents are frequently ambivalent in their attitude to parental support, and the young person's progress towards autonomy is rarely smooth and continuous. But parents, rather than teachers, can best appraise what their child's needs are for parental participation in his school affairs. Teachers who comment 'I never see the parents' seem to be awarding a black mark to the family as a whole. Yet the parents may be making a sensitive assessment of what is an appropriate amount of contact for them to have with the school at a particular stage in their child's school life. Our advocacy here is for the child, and his right to influence and modify the amount of contact between home and secondary school. But even the most dedicated of parents and teachers cannot always be child-centered in their activities. They may want to get something out of parent/teacher encounters for themselves. What is the viability for a relationship of general acquaintance and/of friendship between parent and teacher? Many PTA activities are predicated on the assumption that parents and teachers can do and enjoy each others company. Is this assumption borne out in practice?

A study such as our own, which focusses on the role of the adult (whether parent or teacher) in relation to the child, necessarily underplays the propensities and the self-interest of the adult as an individual. Yet parents, and teachers too, are people, with their own sensitivities. Role-playing cannot fill the bill for an encounter between parents and teacher on an ostensibly social occasion such as a cheese and wine evening. In the absence of their child, it is unnatural for adults to take the role of 'parents' in conversation with other adults, the teachers. Yet it may not be easy for either parents or teachers to muster the social skills necessary for more general conversation with comparative strangers. It is easier for both parents and teachers to get along together as equals when there is a task to be shared, such as running a stall, or building a swimming pool.

Whether or not particular parents and teachers actually get on together socially is more or less fortuitous. Some of the parents interviewed were unequivocal in their comment that social events involving teachers had no attraction for them. But in recognising the right of parents to say that teachers are not the type of people they feel at home with, one must also recognised the teachers' right to admit the same about the parents of their pupils. More than any others, arrangements for this social aspect of parent/teacher contact must leave room for individuality of need and approach, so that possibilities for parent/teacher camaraderie are neither ruled out nor rigidly institutionalised.

One further aspect of the scope available to parents in

their relations with the secondary school remains to be discussed. This is the question of whether parents, as parents, can play a useful part in the government of schools.[7] At the time of writing this is a matter of live debate, and considerable further research is needed to establish both the parameters and the potential of the parent/governor role.

We have already indicated (in Chapter Six) that our research did not encourage us to see a viable role for parents as representatives of other parents. Two of the parents interviewed already were members of the governing boards of the schools their children attended. They found the work rewarding in its opportunities for the expression of their personal and politically affiliated opinions, but the extent to which they could confidently represent the views of other parents seemed in doubt. And those parents who had no experience of participatory democracy, but discussed the role of parent/governor in the abstract, seemed dubious that parents as a body had sufficient in common to authorise specific parents to speak on their behalf.

The 1980 Education Act has however now provided for each school, whether primary or secondary, to have its own governing body, which is to include two parents of pupils at the school. In addition, the act envisages a greater degree of choice by families in which schools their children attend, and the publication of information which will enable that choice to be made from a position of some knowledge about the school's record in recent years.

As we write, the date at which the sections of the act providing for the election of parent (and teacher) governors will be brought into effect for all schools has not yet been announced. The first pupils to be subject to the new admissions procedures will be the cohort of 1982.

Onlookers to social life sometimes claim to perceive a 'new generation' of young people, who, for better or worse, differ in their characteristics, beliefs and behaviour from those who have gone before. It may be that a new generation of parents will be identifiable, who assume and exercise the more active and critical role in relation to their children's schools which the 1980 act envisages for them. Taking a longer view, however, the dictum that 'the more things change, the more they are the same' seems a convincing one. Opportunities for school government and critical consumerism

---

[7]This topic, and a wider set of issues related to the government of education are the subject of research by Johnson and other members of the Educational Studies Unit, Dept. of Government, Brunel University. (*School Governing Bodies* Project, 1980-83).

during the secondary school years will, we predict, be grasped by some parents but will elude the detached majority, whose ideas about relating to the school take little account of educationalists' interpretations and reinterpretations of what the partnership between school and home might be. Yet these parents, like many of those we interviewed, will have aspirations for their children's secondary schooling, and hopes about their children's personal development and achievements. They will try to impart these aspirations and hopes to the child himself, and leave it to him, as part of his growing up, to do what he can to come to acceptable and effective terms with his school.

Cannot the secondary schools drop their preoccupation with 'the home', cease to lament the parents they do not see and concentrate or working effectively with the young people they do see? Such relationship would leave the family where they want to be, in the background, and establish a more realistic partnership between secondary school pupil and school.

Appendix

METHODS OF THE RESEARCH STUDY

FRAMES OF REFERENCE

The interviews with parents on which this book is based formed part of the Schools, Parents and Social Services project, which also investigated the role of welfare agencies in relation to children of secondary school age, and the pastoral work of secondary schools (Johnson et al, 1980). The research design of the project as a whole was based on the premise that the views expressed and accounts given by interview respondents constitute valid data.

It follows from this premise that if, for example, the object is to examine the work of education welfare, the researcher begins by asking an education welfare officer what he does. This straightforward approach has obvious limitations, some of which have been noted in earlier chapters. For some schools of research thought, however, the idea of giving credence to material elicited in interview is quite untenable. Only by 'total immersion' in the institution or occupation under study, or by systematic observation, it is alternatively held, can the researcher gain valid insights and data.

In the field of educational research, both schools of thought have their critics. Without embarking on debate about sociology of knowledge, the two critiques can be only briefly exemplified. On the one hand, research which treats interview material as acceptable data is criticised as an approach which "reifies actors' accounts and places them above any question of their truth and accuracy" (Best, 1980). On the other hand, observational studies which emphasise the researcher's interpretation of (for example) classroom events are rebuked as conveying the "outsider's arrogance". (McNamara, 1980)
For our part, in working as 'outsiders' with teachers and other specialist practitioners, we have preferred the impeachment of naivete to that of arrogance. Reiterated

Appendix

interviews and group discussions enabled some refinement of the original interview statements, but our research account was chiefly based on the purposes expressed and the work patterns described by the professionals concerned. (Johnson et al, 1980)

We have given similar credence to parents' accounts of family experience of the secondary school years. Since so little is known about the way in which parents perceive and relate to the educational institutions their children attend, the first and most obvious thing to do is to ask them about this. The way we set about doing this is fully described in the sections which follow.

The commentary on the secondary school years which this book offers as an outcome of home interviews with parents does not, of course, fully satisfy our thirst for understanding of the relationship between families and institutions. Theorists of the family sometimes give the impression that families can work towards an equilibrium which is undisturbed by outside influences. Practical books on child care dwell on the child in the home. Clinical accounts of family pathology and therapy analyse the intertwining relationships of family members as if the rivalries between generations and the adjustments of adolescence are lived out on a desert island. Yet throughout the family rearing years, most parents go to work, and most children to school. Families live and develop in the context of institutions. Nevertheless, it is easier for individuals to explain and describe their beliefs and behaviour in terms of personal relationships rather than in terms of enmeshment with an institution. (The concept of a parent/teacher relationship seemed more accessible to parents than the concept of a home/school relationship, for example.) The parents' accounts draw alternately on social psychological frames of reference (as when describing their dealings with children or teachers) and administrative frames of reference (as when debating 'rules' for pupil conduct or parental cooperation). Their perception of the impact of the educational institution on the family is therefore fragmented rather than coherent. It is a long-term aid of this and other research by the Educational Studies Unit to move towards a more satisfactory and explanatory analysis of the interplay between individuals and institutions. (*See*, for example, Bird et al, 1981.) Much work remains to be done.

We turn now from this brief conceptual discussion to a detailed account of the parent interview programme, to enable an appraisal of the practicalities of our research approach.

THE SELECTION OF PARENTS

The first constraint on our selection was one of numbers. Because of the need to sustain research dialogues in several

Appendix

agencies at the same time as carrying out home interviews, we decided that the maximum each of the three researchers could achieve would be forty interviews. We briefly considered the possibility of focussing all parent interviews on those parents with a child at a particular stage in secondary school life, for example, all the parents of a particular third year class. We decided against this because it would not necessarily have given us to access to the range of parental experience over the secondary school years which we were hoping for. Parents of third year pupils might also have older children in the school, but they might not.

We also considered approaching rather more parents with children attending the largest of the four schools, scaling down to a smaller number of parents with children at the smallest school. This would have meant an awkward and arbitrary division of labour, since it was from the first agreed that each researcher would interview only parents with pupils at the schools where the researcher had established a collaborative research relationship with teachers. Moreover, there were potentially so many parents at each school whom we might approach that the number of interviews actually aimed for were in any case not claimed to be a proportional sample.

Eventually we decided to try and interview four parents from each of the seven year groups of the four all-through schools focussed on in the study. In this way we would make contact with sixteen parents with children in first year, second year and right through to the seventh (upper sixth) year of secondary school. Many of these parents would of course also have children in other years at the school.[8] These proposed 112 interviews could, conveniently, be almost equally divided between three researchers, without taking them outside the orbit of their 'own' schools.

Given that we could only interview a relatively small number of parents with children at each school, it seemed particularly important to ensure that we made contact with a representative range of parents. We therefore made an analysis of the records of all pupils in one form of each year of every school.[9] We then drew up a 'profile' of the form in terms of apparent parent attitude to the school as revealed in notes to teachers and other correspondence, the apparent behaviour of pupil as indicated in half-yearly reports, the

---

[8] The 109 families we eventually contacted had 328 children between them. 192 of these children were, at the time of the interview, attending secondary school.

[9] Approximately 800 pupil records were studied altogether.

Appendix

child's measured intelligence on leaving primary school and the number of children in the family as indicated by the primary school record card. It was not possible to record all these attributes in all cases, as some pupil records proved sparse and sketchy. (We were soon disabused of our earliest hopes that we might find in the records a note of parental occupations, enabling a selection to be made across a range of occupations. No such information was recorded in the files on any systematic basis.) On the basis of as full a picture as we have been able to build up, we made our selection of four parents across the apparent range of parental attitude and/or pupil behaviour in each form, where possible incorporating a variation in child's measured ability and size of family. We then selected four more 'second string' parents with, so far as possible, similar characteristics. For example, if the 'first choice' parent appeared to have a positive attitude to the school, and had a child of low measured ability, the 'second choice' parent would be selected for the same attributes. In the event, not many of the second choice parents were in fact interviewed. Only 16 parents had declined to be interviewed. When this happened and the researcher was unable to persuade the parent to change his or her mind, the second choice parents with a child in the same year group was approached. Between us, because of the refusals and the two or three parents who had moved from the address listed by the school, we approached 128 families to get out 109 interviews.

LIAISON WITH SCHOOL AND LOCAL AUTHORITY

An essential requirement for the successful completion of our research programme was to enlist and maintain the cooperation, support and approval of the schools and the local authorities.

The possibility, and indeed the inevitability, of what we have come to style a 'flexible' research relationship with schools is something with which researchers in the Educational Studies Unit have increasingly come to terms as they have gained experience. A research design which requires researcher access to teachers, to pupils or, with the cooperation of the school, with parents, must accommodate itself to the organisational styles and communication channels operative in the school in question. It may (or may not) be possible, for example, to require teachers to administer a questionnaire to pupils in a uniform and standardised manner, but it is not possible to require teachers in several different schools to apply identical screening criteria to a selected list of names of pupils whose parents it is proposed to interview. The screening procedure considered appropriate by the school will vary according to who is the principal liaison figure in the school with whom the researchers are in

Appendix

contact, and the persons felt to be most fully aware of the child's home situation, as well as the interpretation which the headteacher places on his own role of overall responsibility for all that goes on in the school.

It would be tedious to detail the differing format of the clearance procedures applied to our lists of proposed interviews in the four schools. In the two schools which had counsellors, these individuals were, as always throughout the research, exceptionally helpful in the thoughtful consideration they gave to the advisability of attempting particular home interviews. In other schools either junior or more senior pastoral teachers - sometimes both - 'vetted' our first and second choice lists, and occasionally suggested which parent it might be most fruitful to approach. Only in four cases were we advised not to approach a particular family, because they were known to be currently experiencing some domestic trauma (serious illness of a child or a parent, or the break up of the home) which would mean that an extended home interview might be inopportune. In no case did teachers attempt to warn us off 'problem' families or families at odds with the school. Rather, they urged us on, and wish us luck in trying to get an interview.

Since some of the names we had selected were of families about which the school knew little, it was inevitable that despite our advance screening we did in fact find ourselves calling on some families who were in trouble. Once having made the contact, it was of course for the families themselves to decide whether a home interview would be a welcome distraction or a last straw. In almost all cases they agreed to be interviewed, sharing their current anxieties as well as their past experiences with the researcher. However, one harrassed father unequivocally declined, saying 'I'm a one parent guy and I'm up to here with it. I've got no time at all.'

Having once screened our list of eight possible interviewees in each year group, this was the last the schools knew of which individuals we actually contacted. We provided each headteacher with a generalised and anonymised written summary of our interviews with parents of pupils from their school, but agreed in advance that we would not inform the school which parents we had in fact interviewed, nor, even if the parents should wish it, would we take up the role of go-between. Some parents were in fact eager to pass complaints through us to the school, but we confined ourselves to advising them which teacher it might be most appropriate for them to contact.

Although we approached parents with the agreement of the schools, our sanction and authorisation for doing so came from our own university and the directors of education of the two local authorities. We each carried two letters of authorisation - one on university letterhead identifying us as

Appendix

a named member of staff at Brunel University, engaged on a particular research project, and the other on local authority letterhead individually authorising us to carry out research enquiries which had the approval of the director of education. No parent in fact asked to see these letters of authorisation, perhaps because we had in all cases written to them a few days before calling.

The approval of the local authority had been negotiated through the steering committees being senior members of the education departments in question. At the conclusion of the research we gave each steering committee a verbal account of our experience in talking to parents.[10] This account was generalised to all four schools, unlike the written reports to headteachers which referred only to the parents of pupils at their school.

THE APPROACH TO THE HOME

About three days before first calling on each parent we sent a duplicated letter on university letterhead addressed to them by name, and individually signed by the researcher proposing to make the call.

We usually sent only three or four of these letters out at a time, so that we could follow them up without too much delay. However, if we were unlucky in finding anyone at home, and made several fruitless calls over a period of a week or two, we would sometimes put a note through the door with a further copy of our original letter, explaining that we had called several times and would be continuing to do so.[11] Very occasionally a parent responded either to the first or second letter by telephoning the university and suggesting an appropriate time for us to call.

Our self-introductory letter was deliberately brief and did not go into detail about our research interests. Parents we interviewed rarely referred to our letter, although, if we

---

[10] All the project documents prepared in collaboration with teachers and agency workers during the research were cleared through the sterring committee, to enable wider circulation and are obtainable from the Educational Studies Unit, Dept. of Government, Brunel University. So far as the work with parents was concerned, it was agreed that the only written outcome would be in the form of published work which protected the anonymity of the parents.

[11] To achieve our 109 interviews we called approximately 350 times at the homes in question.

Appendix

asked them, they usually recalled having received it. It is hard to say how much the letter contributed to our success in getting the interviews, but it seems likely that it did reassure most parents that we were bona fide researchers and not itinerant saleswomen. Once the parent had agreed to be interviewed, the confident trust with which we were welcomed into most homes was impressive.

We realised that many of our interviews would have to take place in the evening, but usually made a first hopeful call during the day, and in a surprisingly large number of cases were fortunate in finding at least one member of the family at home. Contrary to the expectations of maintenance men and parcel-deliverers, even full-time housewives are not always in the house, and in any case the great majority of the mothers we hoped to contact went to work for at least part of the day. But because of the hours they worked, and particularly because many of the fathers and the mothers were employed on shift work, a call at around 10.15 a.m. or 2 p.m. quite often found one or another parent at home, when we could either embark on an immediate interview or arrange another occasion for doing so, when the parent we proposed to interview would be available.

On the question of substitution, we hoped to interview an equal number of fathers and mothers, and our introductory letters were addressed accordingly. In a few cases the individual selected would try to divert us to the other partner, saying they had 'more to do with the school'. This seemed to be said as frequently about fathers as about mothers. However, in most cases we would urge the person originally selected to allow us to interview them, perhaps in the presence of their partner if they felt this would be helpful. Conversely, some parents (usually mothers) who had *not* been selected offered themselves as substitutes, saying that it would be difficult to find their partners at home, or they might not be willing to be interviewed. Unless we were convinced that this was the case we usually avoided substitution and came back again when the other partner was at home. Nevertheless, we occasionally had to accept a substitute, and the slightly greater availability and willingness of wives to be interviewed is evidenced by the fact that 64 of our 109 interviews were arranged with mothers and 45 with fathers. However, both parents were eventually present at a number of the interviews, sharing the discussion.

As we became increasingly involved in the interview programme it became more difficult to space out our calls so that we could carry out an immediate interview if the parent in question happened to be available. We began to have to make calls on our way to or from other interviews, and if we found anyone in make an appointment for a few days time. Most of the evening interviews were arranged in this way, and some parents who were particularly heavily involved in evening

Appendix

shifts or regular social activities fixed an appointment several weeks ahead. (The researcher usually arranged to telephone nearer the time and check that this was still convenient.) A number of older children whom we found at home alone or with friends between 4.30 and 6.00 in the evening cheerfully committed their absent parents to be interviewed at a given time, but appointments made in this way were always offered for renegotiation by the researcher when she met the parent.

GETTING THE INTERVIEW

Home interviews are not easy to obtain, and it would be idle to pretend that we were not apprehensive of failure when we embarked on our programme. By selecting an equal number of 'second string' parents we had made provision for a 50% refusal rate. The interviews which we anticipated would be most difficult to obtain were those where records indicated considerable parents antagonism to the school. We also thought it likely that we would find it more difficult to achieve interviews with fathers than with mothers. Given that, in the event, we had only sixteen refusals, our tactics in obtaining the interviews may be of some interest. Individual differences between the interviewers were of course a factor in the negotiation of each interview, but some generalised points can be made.

We began our interview programme by approaching mothers, with no known history of antagonism to school or education authority. Our intention was to get our hand in with some relatively easy interviews, but the home situation was not always what it seemed. One of the first mothers interviewed proved to be a vocal and active member of a minority religious sect, and the interview rapidly took on proselytising overtones. However, we have to record that the interviewer remained unconverted.

Anti-school parents scarcely over vented their antagonism on the unknown researcher but were often eager to let off steam to an interested listener.

In the majority of cases it was parental diffidence rather than antagonism or hard line attitudes which drew on our negotiating skills. Many of the parents felt initially that they could have little to say to us about their children's secondary education, adding that they did not have much to do with the school. For our part, we rarely brought up the question of which school their child or children attended. Rather we stressed the interest of the university and, where it seemed appropriate, of central government, in the experience of 'ordinary parents' with children at secondary schools.

If the parents considered themselves disqualified for

participation in the research because they rarely went to the school, we emphasised that their views were nevertheless of equal importance with those of parents who were in close touch with it. If they said they were too busy because of heavy family commitments, or thought it inappropriate to participate because their child would soon be leaving school, we stressed the value of their potential contribution to the research because of extensive or extended family life experience. If the obstacle put forward was one of employment and complicated working hours we expressed personal knowledge of such difficulties and took out our diaries.[12]

Although these responses may seem manipulative they were nonetheless sincere, since we genuinely wanted to meet and talk with all the parents on our list, having selected them with such care. As the summer weeks went by and we found ourselves achieving on average about three interviews a week, making about nine calls at different time of day or evening in order to find people at home, we became increasingly motivated to complete our task without sending out additional letters to second string parents or locating new addresses. Towards the end of our list, when one of the all too familiar closed doors eventually opened, we would be on to negotiating the date and time of interview almost before the parent had decided whether he was prepared to take part. However, the tendency towards steamroller tactics which inevitably developed in our negotiation of interviews was always set aside in the interview itself. The pace and length of the encounter was set by the parent, the interviewer willingly adapting to what seemed to suit the parents' inclination and expectations. The fascination and privilege of insights into family life experience never failed to grip us, and as the interview programme continued our encounters with parents proved if anything to be of increasing personal interest and research value.

---

[12] It was during negotiations such as these that we began to appreciate the demands made by shiftwork on family and individual life style. Judgments about the 'fatal immediacy' and propensity for 'instant gratification' of the working class should perhaps be reviewed in the light of the rigorous self-discipline entailed in adapting to alternating shifts. Diary- and calendar-consciousness, were, we found, by no means exclusively middle class attributes.

Appendix

THE SUBSTANCE OF THE INTERVIEW

Our general aim was to elicit parents' perceptions about the role of a parent in the school life of the child, with a particular focus on the secondary school phase. However, in order to see if there was continuity in parental approach in the different stages of school life, we hoped also to enquire into what had been parents' responses to the primary school life of their child.

So far as possible we aimed to keep a balance between getting descriptive accounts from parents about their interaction with the school and obtaining their opinions about the appropriate role of the parent.

In order to achieve some systematic and comparable coverage of parental outlook in each interview, we formulated seven areas of enquiry which we would aim to cover. These were:

> primary school life;
> choice of secondary school;
> preliminary contact with secondary school;
> expectations of the school;
> interaction with the school;
> the parent and the child;
> the parent and outside agencies. [13]

Often there was a topical and appropriate point of departure for the interview, for example, the recent choice of secondary school in the case of a first year child, the imminent school examination of an older pupil, or perhaps some recent encounter with a teacher. In the absence of any positive lead from the parents we would tend to begin with a look back at the primary school years, working on to the present day. We did not use tape recorders and indeed these would have been unsuitable in the far from quiet circumstances in which we often conducted out interviews. Background noises from aircraft, television and other family members would have been too intrusive for effective tape recording. Instead we took notes, using key words or phrases on our clipboards to remind us of areas of enquiry. Questions themselves were always spontaneously formulated to follow the flow of conversation and the parent's and interviewer's styles of

---

[13] By this we meant the various agencies being investigated in other sectors of our research, e.g. education welfare service, child guidance clinic etc.

Appendix

speech.[14]

In a few cases a particularly urgent or topical issue would dominate discussion, for example a parent's dispute with a teacher, or the recent realignment of the parent/child relationship on a one parent family basis. Very occasionally, family life was just too pressing for the full and leisurely exploration of past events. One interview took place within the compass of the preparation and cooking of a pan of chips. But these were the exceptions. Most of the interviews were sufficiently open-ended to enable coverage of all our areas of interest.

WRITING UP THE INTERVIEW

Many difficulties present themselves in writing up a number of unstructured interviews in comparable and collatable form. We feel we met this challenge with some success.

Elizabeth Ransom devised a 'grid' of fourteen sheets which was duplicated in appropriate quantities. The sheets were unequally and, as it proved, more or less appropriately divided between our seven areas of interest (for example, one for parents and agencies and one for choice of secondary school, but six for interaction with the school - an umbrella type topic potentially covering many aspects of home/school relationship). Each sheet was further sub-divided into particular topics of interest or open comment sections.

After each interview we would write up our notes on these grids, slotting our information into the various sections, repeating or cross-referencing it where appropriate. Parents were identified only by a pre-arranged code.

An hour long interview took approximately three hours to write out in this way. At the time when interviews were at

---

[14] While the interviewer made no attempt to imitate or adopt the vocabulary of the parent, care was taken not to introduce educational jargon or unfamiliar terms. One or two unexpected difficulties of communication presented themselves however, as for example the use of the generic term 'secondary' school. One mother felt herself to be ineligible for interview because 'they all go to these *comprehensives* now'.

All the more lengthy quotations in this book were noted by one interviewer. Whilst not verbatim in the strictest sense, they convey the gist, sequence and vocabulary of the original communication.

Appendix

their height, much of the weekend was spent in writing up. We felt the task worthwhile in that little hard won information was lost, and writing up provided an on-going opportunity to mull over the interview while it was still relatively fresh in the mind of the interviewer. However, the completed grids were fairly densely packed with information in idiosyncratic handwriting. A further chore, to ensure the mutual availability of the data, was reading the sectionalised information onto tape, for typing up in systematised form. This final process proved tedious and time-consuming. In retrospect it seems clear that some short cuts should have been found. At the time, the interviews were proceeding in between much other demanding fieldwork, also requiring analysis, and we did the best we could. We are not too dissatisfied with our rather cumbersome solution to the problem of structuring unstructured data.

RESEARCHERS AND RESEARCHED

"Who were the interviewers?" is a legitimate question to ask in appraising any interview-based research. The authors of this book, with Katherine Bowden, were the interviewers in question and it would embarrass us to attempt too detailed a description of ourselves. However, some information is necessary.

All the interviewers were at the time of the research graduates of some years standing, with varied experience of social research. The principal difference between us was one of age and family experience, one of the trio being middle-aged with a grown up daughter, and the other two being married women in their late twenties, as yet without children.

Little noticeable difference in response to the interviewer is apparent to us from our interview accounts. However, it does seem that parents may have talked more readily to Daphne Johnson about the ups and downs of family life with adolescent children, while Elizabeth Ransom and Katherine Bowden heard rather more about parents' encounters with the young teachers whom these interviewers much resembled.

The parents themselves were mostly in their late thirties, living in those parts of Hounslow and Hillingdon which lie in the shadow of London Airport, nearly all in local authority-built housing. The five 'vignettes' in chapter one convey some impression of the range of parents contacted.

It was never our intention to base our study on a class categorisation. Rather, our analysis was one of family context. The criterion of eligibility for interview was that one or more children in the family was a pupil at one of four comprehensive schools. While the schools did not have rigidly enforced catchment areas, most pupils lived in the

Appendix

neighbourhood of the school they attended.

We did not ask the parents what work they did, but many of them told us. The great majority of these were in manual work. A few were self-employed. The range of occupations mentioned by fathers included van driver, bus driver, policeman, fireman, assembly worker, maintenance engineer, self-employed builder. Of greater interest to us than their actual occupations were their hours of work. As indicated in the main text of this book, many worked a shift system.

The majority of the mothers were in employment, usually on a part-time basis. Their jobs were for the most part in local factories, hospitals, shops or the school meals service. A few were in clerical employment.

Nine of the parents interviewed told us they were widowed, separated or divorced. Seven of the families were from ethnic minority groups. Parents and adolescent children in most of these families had been born outside the United Kingdom.

In all cases we asked about number of children in the family. Overall, family size in the 109 families was above the national average, and this was the case for the schools' clientele as a whole, not just the parents we interviewed. The table below shows the distribution of family size among the 109 families contacted.

Number of children in family	Number of families
1 child	11
2 children	41
3 children	25
4 children	15
5 children	10
6 or more children	7

While most of the parents of large families were older than the apparent modal age of thirty-six or thirty-seven, this was not always the case. One mother of eight had had her first child at the age of seventeen, and was still only thirty-seven.

Some older parents had had only an elementary education. Most of the parents, however, had been at secondary modern schools. About a quarter of the parents mentioned that one or other of them had attended one of the comprehensive schools under study, in an earlier secondary modern form.

Bibliography of works referenced in the text

Annual Report of the National Society for Promoting the Education of the Poor in the Principles of the Established Church, 1844.

Best, R. (Book Review), *British Educational Research Journal*, Vol 6, No 2, 1980.

Bird, C., Chessum, R., Furlong, J. and Johnson, D. (ed) *Disaffected Pupils*. A report to the Department of Education and Science, Brunel University, 1981.

Blyth, W., "Some relationships between homes and schools" in Craft et al (eds), *Linking Home and School*, Longman, 1967.

Craft, M., Raynor, J., Cohen, L. (eds), *Linking Home and School*. Longman 1967, 2nd Edition, 1972, 3rd Edition, Harper and Row, 1980.

Davies, B., *Universality, Selectivity and Effectiveness in Social Policy*, Heinemann, 1978.

Davis, A., *Social class influence on learning*. University of Chicago Press, 1950.

Douglas, J. W. B., *The Home and the School - a study of ability and attainment in the primary school*, MacGibbon & Kee, 1964.

Fitzherbert, K., *Child Care Services and the Teacher*, Maurice Temple Smith, 1977.

Floud, J., "Social class factors in educational achievement" in Halsey, A. H. (ed), *Ability and Educational Opportunity*, OECD, 1961.

Fraser, E., *Home Environment and the School*, University of London Press (Scottish Council for Research in Education, Publication No 43), 1959.

Goodacre, E. J., *Teachers and Their Pupils' Home Backgrounds*, NFER, 1968.

Halsey, A. H., Floud, J. and Anderson, C. Arnold (eds), *Education, Economy and Society: A Reader in the Sociology of Education*, Free Press of Glencoe, 1961.

Halsey, A. H. (ed), *Ability and Educational Opportunity*, OECD, 1961.

HMSO publications:

A New Partnership for Our Schools (Taylor Report), Department of Education and Science and Welsh Officer, 1977.

Children and Their Primary Schools (Plowden Report), 1967 (CAC).

Early Leaving (Gurney-Dixon Report), 1954 (CAC).

Fifteen to Eighteen (Crowther Report), 1959 (CAC).

Half our Future (Newsom Report), 1963 (CAC).

Higher Education (Robbins Report) Cmnd. 2154, 1963.

Parent/Teacher Relations in Primary Schools (Education Survey No 5), 1968.

Report of Inter-Departmental Committee on Physical Deterioration, Cmnd. 2175, 1904.

Teachers and Parents, Report No 41 to the Department of Education and science, 1967.

Johnson, D. Ransom, E., Packwood, T., Bowden, K. and Kogan, M., *Secondary Schools and the Welfare Network*, Allen and Unwin, 1980.

Johnson, D., "Home-School Relations, 1970-1980" in Cohen, L., Manion, L. and Thomas, J., *Educational Research and Development in Great Britain*, NFER/Nelson, 1982.

Lynch, J. and Pimlott, J., *Parents and Teachers*, Macmillan, 1976.

Mays, J. B., 1962, *Education and the Urban Child*, Liverpool University Press, 1962.

Mays, J. B., "The impact of neighbourhood values" in Craft, M. et al (eds) *Linking Home and School*, Longman, 1967.

McGeeney, P., *Parents are Welcome*, Longman, 1969.

McNamara, D. R., "The outsider's arrogance: the failure of participant observers to understand classroom events" in *British Educational Research Journal*, Vol 6, No 2, 1980.

Morton Williams, R., The 1964 National Survey: survey among parents of primary school children, Appendix 3 in *Children and Their Primary Schools*, Vol 2, Research and Surveys (Plowden Report), HMSO, 1967.

Nisbet, J., "Family environment and intelligence" in Eugenics Review, XLV, 1953.

Pinker, R., *Social Theory and Social Policy*, Heinemann, 1971.

Robinson, M., *Schools and Social Work*, Routledge and Kegan Paul, 1978.

Shipman, M., *The Sociology of the School*, Longman, 1968.

Titmuss, R., *Commitment to Welfare*, Allen and Unwin, 1968.

Wiseman, S., *Education and Environment*, Manchester University Press, 1964.

Young, M. and McGeeney, P., *Learning Begins at Home: A Study of a Junior School and its Parents*, Routledge and Kegan Paul, 1968.

INDEX

ACE 23, 24
Attendance
 school 83-88, 101-105, 122; see also Truancy
 by parents at school events 2, 21, 53, 58-61, 137
Best 129
Bird 130
Blyth 19, 20

Careers Guidance 13, 78, 94, 105-110; see also Careers Service
Careers Service 18, 97, 105-110
CASE 23, 25
Child Guidance Clinic/Service 97, 111
Child Psychiatrists 3, 80
choice of secondary school 2, 7, 37-45, 66, 138
Cohen 119
community schools 24-25
concerts (school) 61-62
Crowther Report 19
curriculum 39, 64, 93

Davies 98
Davis 20
dependency 2, 6, 71, 74-75, 118
discipline 7, 39, 40, 65, 73-76, 79-81
 self discipline 9

Douglas 21

Education Act
 1944 19, 26;
 1980 2, 27, 127
Education Department 15, 41, 88, 97, 104, 105; see also local authority
Education Office - see education department
education psychologists 3, 25, 97
education welfare officers 3, 22, 25, 88, 97, 101-105, 123
Education Welfare Service 16, 97, 101-105, 111, 138
examinations (exams) 11, 66, 76, 108, 109
expectations, parents of secondary schools 12-13, 16, 31, 43, 45-9, 138
 parents of contacts between home and school 2, 54, 58, 61-7, 82, 120
 teachers of contacts between home and school 2, 50-53, 56, 71, 82

financial help for the school 7, 91, 119
Fitzherbert 25, 110
Floud 19, 52
Fraser 19

145

grammar school(s) 7, 10, 11, 14-15, 37-43, 110

Halsey 19, 20, 52
headmaster 7, 87
headmistress 35
headteacher 8, 23, 34, 36, 38, 40, 61, 67-68, 92, 133
health, children's 36, 40, 84-86, 98-100, 102, 111, 118
Home and School Council 23
home interviews 3-5, 16, 53, 129-141
home visiting 21, 24, 51, 122-124
homework 7, 9, 13, 66, 69, 83, 88-89, 122

immigrant families 5, 123, description of one family 12-14, ethnic minority groups 4, 141
information exchange 90-91

job skills 13, 46, 48
Johnson 3, 5, 97, 107, 119, 124, 127, 129, 130
Juvenile Bureau 97-98

Local authority 8, 16, 26, 35, 42, 44, 92, 132-134
Local Education Authority see local authority
Lynch 58, 61

mathematics (Maths) 13, 55, 66, 92, 95
Mays 21-22
McGeeney 24
McNamara 129
Midwinter 24

National Society 18
newsletter 80
Newsom Report 19
Nisbet 19

open days 40, 79
open evenings 7, 22, 50, 78

option choice 11, 50, 59, 66, 93

parent governors 25-26, 44, 93, 127
parents associations (PTAs) 2, 4, 11, 22-23, 25, 50, 63-65, 77, 79, 81, 91-93, 119, 126
parents evenings 11, 15, 22, 50, 54-61, 79, 80, 120-121, 124, 125
parents' role 9-10, 70-82, 91-96, 138
Parent-Teacher Associations see parents associations
pastoral systems 67
physical education (PE) 66
Pinker 98
Plowden Report 1, 23
police 112, account of a police officer's family 8-9; see also juvenile bureau
poverty 18
primary school(s) 2, 8, 10, 16, 21, 23, 31-39, 44, 63, 71, 75-78, 81, 86, 93, 111, 117, 138
primary school teachers 34-36, 118

records, school, 90, 131
religious and moral education 26, 49, 74
reports, school, 50, 54-55, 57-59
Robinson 25

school counsellor 15, 25, 113
school governor(s) 25, 51; see also parent governors
School Health Service 16, 97-100, 111; School Medical Service 18
school meals 18, 35, 93
school plays 61-62
school psychological service 97, 111 see also education psychologists

school secretary 68
secondary modern schools 6,
  15, 39, 42, 43
sex discrimination 45-46
shift work 9, 14, 53, 60, 61,
  102, 135, 137
Shipman 92
single parent 9-12, 60, 133,
  139
sixth form 13, 88, 101,
  109-110
social class, the influence of
  class on relationships with
  school, 4, 18-22, 53,
  60-61, 96, 140-141
social workers 111-112; school
  social workers 3, 25, 105
sports days 61
subject teaching 9, 43, 47,
  57, 64, 66, 89

Taylor Committee Report 26-27
technical college 95
television 5, 138
Titmuss 98
truancy 41, 56, 65, 71, 79,
  83-88, 98-105; see also
  attendance

uniform 93, 101

welfare agencies 3, 96, 97-114
Wiseman 20

Youth and Community Service 97

For Product Safety Concerns and Information please contact our EU representative GPSR@taylorandfrancis.com
Taylor & Francis Verlag GmbH, Kaufingerstraße 24, 80331 München, Germany

www.ingramcontent.com/pod-product-compliance
Lightning Source LLC
Chambersburg PA
CBHW050553300426
44112CB00013B/1901